Hong Kong

PUBLIC WORLDS

Dilip Gaonkar and Benjamin Lee

Series Editors

A C K B A R   A B B A S

Hong Kong

Culture and the

Politics of Disappearance

PUBLIC WORLDS, VOLUME 2

UNIVERSITY OF MINNESOTA PRESS

MINNEAPOLIS   LONDON

Grateful acknowledgment is made for permission to reprint from the following:
Edmund Blunden, *A Hong Kong House* (London: HarperCollins, 1962); Louise Ho, *Local Habitation* (Hong Kong: Twilight Books, 1994); Leung Ping-Kwan, *City at the End of Time*, trans. Gordon Osing (Hong Kong: Twilight Books, 1992).

Published by the University of Minnesota Press
111 Third Avenue South, Suite 290, Minneapolis, MN 55401-2520
Printed in the United States of America on acid-free paper

Fourth printing, 2008

Library of Congress Cataloging-in-Publication Data
Abbas, M. A. (M. Ackbar)
    Hong Kong : culture and the politics of disappearance / Ackbar
Abbas.
        p.   cm. — (Public worlds ; v. 2)
    Includes bibliographical references (p.   ) and index.
    ISBN 978-0-8166-5025-5 (hard : alk. paper). — ISBN 978-0-8166-5026-2
(pbk. : alk. paper)
    1. Hong Kong—Civilization.   2. Hong Kong—History—Transfer of
Sovereignty to China, 1997.   I. Title   II. Series.
DS796.H75A34   1997
951.25—dc20   96-41269

Contents

Acknowledgments

I would like to thank Benjamin Lee, that great enabler, and the Center for Transcultural Studies for providing a space where many of the ideas for this book were first aired. I am also grateful to Kathleen Woodward and the Center for Twentieth Century Studies for many kindnesses.

Some sections of this book have appeared, in a different form, in *Positions*, *Discourse*, and *Public Culture*. I would like to thank the editors of these journals for their interest in my work.

1

Introduction: Culture in a Space of Disappearance

Living in interesting times is a dubious advantage, in fact, a curse according to an old Chinese saying. Interesting times are periods of violent transitions and uncertainty. People in Hong Kong, faced with the prospect of 1997, clearly live in interesting times. The city's history has always followed an unexpected course—from fishing village to British colony to global city to one of China's Special Administrative Regions, from 1 July 1997, onward. "With cities, it is as with dreams: everything imaginable can be dreamed," Italo Calvino's Marco Polo asserts, in a remark strikingly apropos of Hong Kong. "But even the most unexpected dream is a rebus that conceals a desire or, its reverse, a fear."[1] Cultural forms, too, can perhaps also be regarded as a rebus that projects a city's desires and fears, although it is likely to be a rebus of a particularly complex kind. This book concerns the manifold relations between cultural forms in Hong Kong—particularly cinema, architecture, and writing—and the changing cultural space of the city. It will not give a general and exhaustive survey of these cultural forms but will use them to pursue a particular theme: the cultural self-invention of the Hong Kong subject in a cultural space that I will be calling a space of disappearance.

Any discussion of Hong Kong culture must sooner or later raise the question of its relation to colonialism. But *colonialism*, at least in Hong

Kong, is less an explanatory term than a term that needs explaining. There are a number of factors specific to Hong Kong that must be considered in a discussion of colonialism. For example, in contrast to other colonial cities (say, in India, Africa, or South America) Hong Kong has no precolonial past to speak of. It is true that in a sense Hong Kong did have a history before 1841, when it was ceded to the British; there are records of human settlement on the island going back at least to the Sung dynasty; but the history of Hong Kong, in terms that are relevant to what it has become today, has effectively been a history of colonialism. Another point to note is that while 98 percent of the population is ethnic Chinese, history (both colonial history and history on the mainland) has seen to it that the Hong Kong Chinese are now culturally and politically quite distinct from mainlanders; two peoples separated by a common ethnicity, a first example of disappearance. This has produced many instances of mutual mistrust and misunderstanding, with one side demonizing the other. It is not true, as some might wish to believe, that if you scratch the surface of a Hong Kong person you will find a Chinese identity waiting to be reborn. The Hong Kong person is now a bird of a different feather, perhaps a kind of Maltese Falcon. This suggests that 1997 will not be simply the moment of liberation from colonial rule; it will also mark a moment of transition to a form of governance that has no clear historical precedents.

Besides these already quite complex local and specific factors that are relevant to colonialism in Hong Kong, there are also wider issues to bear in mind, particularly the fact that on a world scale colonialism itself is a changing paradigm that takes one form in the era of imperialism and a different and more paradoxical form in the era of globalism. The original title of this book was *The Last Emporium*, a title that calls attention, perhaps a little too obliquely, to this changing paradigm in relation to Hong Kong. It points not only to the end of empire, to the fact that Hong Kong is formally one of Britain's last colonies in the old-fashioned sense; it is also meant to suggest more indirectly that the end of empire does not mean the end of capitalism (of which imperialism was one manifestation), merely that capitalism has entered a new phase. In other words, 1997 will not mark the double demise of capitalism and colonialism. The last emporium will be, and in fact already has been, replaced by other forms produced by a mutation in the capitalist system. Such a mutation has been variously described. For example, Scott Lash and John Urry see it as a movement from "organised capitalism" to what they call "disorganised capital," while Manuel Castells thinks of it as a movement toward the space of flows of the "informational city."[2] Most accounts, however, put the stress on the fluidity, flexibility, and decentralized nature of the new form of capital. The Hong Kong economy has benefited very much from these developments that have allowed it to change from a trading post in the nineteenth century to its present position as a premier financial center of Southeast Asia, from a colonial city to a global city.

In this respect, the intriguing argument put forward by Anthony King of a connection between the colonial city and the global city deserves serious consideration. He points out that it is colonialism itself that has pioneered methods of incorporating precapitalist, preindustrial, and non-European societies into the world economy and found ways of dealing with ethnically, racially, and culturally different societies. The surprising consequence of this "historically significant phenomenon" is that "colonial cities can be viewed as the *forerunners* of what the contemporary capitalist world city would eventually become."[3] One of the implications of this argument is that *colonialism* in a number of instances is the surprising middle term that allows imperialism to make the leap to globalism. It is imperialism that produces by definition the colonial city, but the colonial city can also prefigure the global city. The rise of globalism spells the end of the old empires, but not before the offsprings of these empires, the previous colonial cities, have been primed to perform well as global cities. This makes it possible to explain why, with the end of imperialism, colonialism could take a global form, and why it could decisively abandon the old imperial attitudes and even take on benign characteristics, as in the case of Hong Kong, thus seeming to contradict more orthodox understandings of colonialism as necessarily exploitative. The presence of these strange historical loops implies a more complex kind of colonial space produced by the unclean breaks and unclear connections between imperialism and globalism, which is how colonialism in Hong Kong must now be considered. This in turn has important consequences for the study of Hong Kong culture: culture in Hong Kong cannot just be related to "colonialism"; it must be related to this changed and changing space, this colonial space of disappearance, which in many respects does not resemble the old colonialisms at all.

There is, however, yet another factor to consider. Just at the moment in the late seventies and early eighties when Hong Kong seemed to have successfully remade itself into a global city, the situation took a new turn. It was at this juncture that China reclaimed Hong Kong, as if it were a new Atlantis. In 1984, with the signing of the Sino-British Joint Declaration returning Hong Kong to Chinese rule in 1997, the long goodbye of Britain to its "last emporium" began in earnest. It is with cultural changes taking place in Hong Kong during this critical period, intimately related to social and political changes, that we will be concerned. It is possible to think of this period as a period when an "older" but still operative politics of national legitimacy and geophysical boundaries comes into conflict with a "newer" politics of global flows, information, and the devalorization of physical boundaries. But it is also possible to think of the period as a time *when categories like "old" and "new" lose some of their force*, as the old forms are placed in new configurations. This amounts to saying that the cultural space of Hong Kong now presents us with a number of unusual and even paradoxical features, some of which I shall try to describe in a preliminary way.

. To begin with, there is the uneasy relationship between remaining content with a "floating" identity that has served Hong Kong so well in the past, and the need to establish something more definite in response to current political exigencies. Hong Kong has up to quite recently been a city of transients. Much of the population was made up of refugees or expatriates who thought of Hong Kong as a temporary stop, no matter how long they stayed. The sense of the temporary is very strong, even if it can be entirely counterfactual. The city is not so much a place as a space of transit. It has always been, and will perhaps always be, a port in the most literal sense—a doorway, a point in between—even though the nature of the port has changed. A port city that used to be located at the intersections of different spaces, Hong Kong will increasingly be at the intersections of different times or speeds. There are already signs of this happening. It is not by accident that the largest current project is the construction of the new airport on Lantau, one of Hong Kong's outlying islands. When completed, the airport will be a kind of city within a city, but a city without citizens, a semiotic or informational city populated by travelers and service personnel. For the port mentality, everything is provisional, ad hoc; everything floats—currencies, values, human relations. But such a mentality was only viable before anxieties over 1997, and before events at Tiananmen 1989. Now faced with the uncomfortable possibility of an alien identity about to be imposed on it from China, Hong Kong is experiencing a kind of last-minute collective search for a more definite identity.

A second observation on Hong Kong's cultural space concerns what I would like to call decadence and its relationship to the development of Hong Kong culture. There is something about Hong Kong's famous "energy and vitality" that could be related to decadence—a useful concept once it is shorn of all moralistic and fin de siècle overtones. The energy here is an energy that gets largely channeled into one direction: that is what I understand by decadence. One of the effects of a very efficient colonial administration is that it provides almost no outlet for political idealism (until perhaps quite recently); as a result, most of the energy is directed toward the economic sphere. Historical imagination, the citizens' belief that they might have a hand in shaping their own history, gets replaced by speculation on the property or stock markets, or by an obsession with fashion or consumerism. If you cannot choose your political leaders, you can at least choose your own clothes. We find therefore not an atmosphere of doom and gloom, but the more paradoxical phenomenon of *doom and boom*: the more frustrated or blocked the aspirations to "democracy" are, the more the market booms. By the same logic, the only form of political idealism that has a chance is that which can go together with economic self-interest, when "freedom," for example, could be made synonymous with the "free market." This, I believe, is how one can understand the unprecedented mass demonstrations over the Tiananmen Massacre by the hundreds of thousands of the middle class who had never before marched in the streets. June 1989 in Hong Kong was a rare moment when economic self-interest could so easily misrecognize itself as political idealism. There was certainly genuine emotion and outrage, which does not preclude the possibility that many of the marchers were moved by how much they were moved. In any event, the patriotic fervor in most cases was short-lived and without political outcome. In the aftermath to Tiananmen, amazingly complacent bumper stickers appeared for a while decorating the automobiles of the bourgeoisie, which read: "Motoring in dignity, for freedom and democracy." If the situation I have been describing can be called decadent, it is decadent not in the sense of decline (because we see what looks like progress everywhere) but in the sense of a one-dimensional development in a closed field. It is such decadence that has made it difficult to recognize the existence of a Hong Kong culture.

A third point involves the strange dialectic between autonomy and dependency that we see in Hong Kong's relation both to Britain and China. The end of British rule in Hong Kong and the passing of sovereignty back into the hands of China is not a simple return of Chinese territory to the Chinese. Ironically, it is Hong Kong's colonial history, the only history it has known and a history that cannot be forgotten overnight, that has distanced Hong Kong culturally and politically from China and that will make their relationship not simply one of reunification. When sovereignty reverts to China, we may expect to find a situation that is quasi-colonial, but with an important historical twist: the colonized state, while politically subordinate, is in many other crucial respects *not* in a dependent subaltern position but is in fact more advanced—in terms of education, technology, access to international networks, and so forth—than the colonizing state. This amounts to saying that colonialism will not merely be Hong Kong's chronic condition; it will be accompanied by displaced chronologies or achronicities. Such a situation may well be unprecedented in the history of colonialism, and it might justify the use of the term *postcoloniality* in a special sense: a postcoloniality that precedes decolonization. Some foreshadowings are already evident in Hong Kong's present relation to Britain: it is the Hong Kong and Shanghai Bank that has recently taken over the British Midlands Bank and not vice versa. As for China, administering the Hong Kong "special administrative region" after 1997 may be for the Chinese authorities a little like handling a gadget from the future. For example, one of the hiccups about the new airport, besides the huge cost, is anxiety on the Chinese side about whether they will be able to handle the extremely high-tech sophistication of the project. The historical ironies will only become more accentuated as China continues on its reformist course, as it looks likely to do, making the formula of "one country, two systems" so much more easy to dismantle: what we will find will not be two systems (socialist, capitalist) but one system at different stages of development—a difference in times and speeds.

Finally, perhaps the most striking feature of all about Hong Kong's cultural space today is the radically changed status of culture itself. One of the effects of colonialism was that until as late as the seventies, Hong Kong did not realize it could have a culture. The import mentality saw culture, like everything else, as that which came from elsewhere: from Chinese tradition, more legitimately located in mainland China and Taiwan, or from the West. As for Hong Kong, it was, in a favorite phrase, "a cultural desert." Not that there was nothing going on in cinema, architecture, and writing; it was just not recognized to be culture as such. This refusal to see what is there is an example of reverse hallucination, or what Sigmund Freud in his essay on Wilhelm Jensen's "Gradiva" called "negative hallucination." If hallucination means seeing ghosts and apparitions, that is, something that is not there, reverse hallucination means *not* seeing what *is* there. Thus Norbert Hanold the archaeologist, obsessed with the Greek statue Gradiva who walks with a particular gait, cannot see the living woman Zoe Bertgang: "Hanold, who . . . had the gift of 'negative hallucination,' who possessed the art of not seeing and not recognizing people who were actually present."[4] What changed the largely negative attitude to Hong Kong culture was not just Hong Kong's growing affluence; more important, it was the double trauma of the signing of the Sino-British Joint Declaration of

1984 followed by the Tiananmen Massacre of 1989. These two events confirmed a lot of people's fears that the Hong Kong way of life with its mixture of colonialist and democratic trappings was in imminent danger of disappearing. "Anything about which one knows that one soon will not have it around becomes an image," Walter Benjamin wrote.[5] The imminence of its disappearance, I would argue, was what precipitated an intense and unprecedented interest in Hong Kong culture. The anticipated end of Hong Kong as people knew it was the beginning of a profound concern with its historical and cultural specificity. But then the cause of this interest in Hong Kong culture—1997—may also cause its demise. The change in status of culture in Hong Kong can be described as follows: from reverse hallucination, which sees only desert, to a culture of disappearance, whose appearance is posited on the imminence of its disappearance.

These remarks can be compared with some points that Fredric Jameson makes toward the end of his essay on postmodernism about the new status of culture in relation to social life today:

> Everything in the previous discussion suggests that what we have been calling postmodernism is inseparable from, and unthinkable without the hypothesis of, some fundamental mutation of the sphere of culture in the world of late capitalism, which includes a momentous modification of its social function. . . . Yet to argue that culture is today no longer endowed with the relative autonomy it once enjoyed as one level among others in earlier moments of capitalism (let alone in precapitalist societies) is not necessarily to imply its disappearance or extinction. Quite the contrary; we must go on to affirm that the dissolution of an autonomous sphere of culture is rather to be imagined in terms of an explosion: a prodigious expansion of culture throughout the social realm, to the point at which everything in our social life—from economic value and state power to practices and to the very structure of the psyche itself—can be said to have become "cultural" in some original and yet untheorized sense.[6]

In the case of Hong Kong, there has indeed been "an expansion of culture throughout the social realm" amounting to an "explosion." We are witnessing certainly not the disappearance of culture, but "some original and yet untheorized" form of culture, what I propose to describe as *a culture of disappearance*. This requires a preliminary word of explanation.

In the first place, disappearance here does not imply nonappearance, absence, or lack of presence. It is not even nonrecognition—it is more a question of misrecognition, of recognizing a thing as something else. One of the clearest examples, if one can put it this way, of this first sense of disappearance is what we have discussed as reverse hallucination, which as we shall see in subsequent chapters is not restricted to an earlier phase of Hong Kong culture but is still with us today. There is something very definite about dis-appearance, a kind of pathology of presence. This brings us to our second point about disappearance, its relationship to representation, including questions of self-representation. For example, if Hong Kong is now a focus of attention because its very existence is under threat, nevertheless, the way the city has been made to appear in many representations in fact works to make it disappear, most perniciously through the use of old binaries like East-West "differences." We will see many instances of this in cinema, architecture, and writing, where disappearance is not a matter of effacement but of replacement and substitution, where the perceived danger is recontained through representations that are familiar and plausible. But there is also a third sense of disappearance that we find in the innovative examples of Hong Kong culture, which accounts to a large extent for why Hong Kong cultural productions today are in a position to be so provocative and exciting to an international audience: we only have to think of filmmakers like Stanley Kwan and Wong Kar-wai. This third aspect of disappearance consists of developing techniques of disappearance that respond to, without being absorbed by, a space of disappearance. These are not techniques that go against disappearance; they cannot even be usefully thought of in terms of "critical strategies of resistance." Rather, it is a question of working with disappearance and taking it elsewhere, of using disappearance to deal with disappearance. For example, if reverse hallucination is the problem, then Stanley Kwan will use the figure of a ghost in his film *Rouge* to reverse these reversals. If visual representations make images disappear in clichés, it will be a matter of inventing a form of visuality that problematizes the visual, as in the films of Wong Kar-wai.

It is also possible to situate the concept of disappearance that I am developing in terms of textual, social, and urban theory, which will allow us to touch on three other aspects of this elusive concept: its relation to the ephemeral, to speed, and to abstraction.

We can introduce the relation of disappearance to the ephemeral by considering Louis Aragon's novel *Paris Peasant*, a text that so impressed Benjamin. Speaking about the Paris arcades that were fast disappearing as a result of modern city planning in terms that would seem at first sight quite relevant to present-day Hong Kong, he wrote: "It is only today, when the pickaxe menaces them, that they have at last become the true sanctuaries of a cult of the ephemeral. . . . Places that were incomprehensible yesterday, and that tomorrow will never know."[7] What Aragon calls the cult of the ephemeral is a mode of attention directed at a disappearing space, a way of understanding what he called "the disquieting atmosphere of places . . . peopled with unrecognised sphinxes." This would lead to an allegorical reading of space that attends not only to what is there but also to what is no longer or not yet there. The sense of the ephemeral that might have still sufficed for Paris in the 1920s, however, can no longer deal with the kinds of changes that take place in present-day Hong Kong, where we come across phenomena that do not merely disturb our sense of time but that completely upset and reverse it. For example, the apparently permanent—like buildings and even whole towns—can be temporary, while the temporary—like abode in Hong Kong—could be very permanent.

To explain phenomena like these, we need something more than Aragon's cult of the ephemeral or the reflective looking before and after of allegory. We need something like Paul Virilio's argument about the relation of disappearance to speed, the kind of speed that comes in the wake of electronic technology and the mediatization of the real, and the spatial distortions produced by this kind of speed. In *The Lost Dimension*, Virilio describes how under conditions of speed our concept of physical dimensions loses all meaning through sensory overload, the fusion and confusion of the fast and the slow, the absence of transition between the big and the small. The result is the breakdown of the analogical in favor of the digital, the preference for the abstract dot (the pixel) over the analogical line, plane, or solid. "In this most recent experience of space that upsets the order of the visible that began in the Quattrocento," Virilio writes, "we are directly or indirectly witnessing a kind of tele-conquest of appearance."[8] Disappearance then is a consequence of speed.

We come finally to the relation between disappearance and abstraction that is implied in Henri Lefebvre's concept of social space.[9] We can approach the argument through Virilio. One consequence of the "tele-conquest of appearance" is that something happens to our experience of space. It becomes more varied and multifarious, oversaturated with signs and images, at the same time as it becomes more abstract and ungraspable. This brings us to the relation between disappearance and abstraction, to abstraction as the contemporary mode of disappearance. Consider as one aspect of this problematic the status of the image. The more abstract the space, the more important the image becomes (a point the Situationists also made), and the more dominant becomes the visual as a mode. This relation between abstraction and the image, however, must be understood in a specific way. The image is not a compensation for abstraction, an amelioration of its lack of the concrete; rather, it is the "concrete" form that abstraction now takes, what Lefebvre calls a "concrete abstraction." This paradox of a "richness" and "concreteness" that go together with abstraction is also the paradox of disappearance, which we can now suggest is of crucial importance to an understanding of social space, in Hong Kong as much as elsewhere.

If disappearance problematizes representation, it also problematizes self-representation. A central issue that Hong Kong culture implicitly or explicitly poses is the question of subjectivity in a space of disappearance. What happens to our subjectivity under these conditions? The problem is usually posed more misleadingly as a question of "Hong Kong identity" or "postcolonial identity."

In the case of Hong Kong, and for reasons already given, postcoloniality can only be understood in a nonliteralist sense. Postcoloniality does not take the physical departure of the colonial power (or even the subject's own departure) as its point of origin, just as colonialism in its effects does not end with the signing of a treaty. Postcoloniality begins, it has already begun, when subjects find themselves thinking and acting in a certain way; in other words, postcoloniality is a tactic and a practice, not a legal-political contract, or a historical accident. It means finding ways of operating under a set of difficult conditions that threatens to appropriate us as subjects, an appropriation that can work just as well by way of acceptance as it can by rejection. Dealing with such conditions may involve, for example, thinking about emigration in a certain way, emigration not in the diasporic sense of finding another space, of relocating, with all the pathos of departure, but in the sense of remaking a given space that for whatever reason one cannot leave, of dis-locating—emigration, that is to say, before the exit visas have been issued. In this regard, it is worth considering Gilles Deleuze and Félix Guattari's distinction between the nomad and the migrant. The nomad, they point out, is essentially different from the migrant who moves *elsewhere*, while it is

> false to define the nomad by movement. [Arnold] Toynbee is profoundly right to suggest that the nomad is on the contrary *he who does not move.* Whereas the migrant leaves behind a milieu that has become amorphous or hostile, the nomad is one who does not depart, does not want to depart, who clings to the smooth space left by the receding forest, where the steppe or the desert advance, and who invents nomadism as a response to this challenge.[10]

Migrant and nomad are two very different forms of disappearance and different ways of dealing with it.

Another problem with the question of postcolonial identity in Hong Kong is that it cannot be usefully posed by taking our bearings from the old binarisms (like the difference between "East" and "West," "tradition" and "modernity," and other similarly moldy chestnuts)—if for no other reason because the local and the global are becoming more and more intimately imbricated with each other. In fact, the available binarisms tend to confuse more than they clarify questions of identity. To take one example, Hong Kong culture cannot simply mean focusing on Hong Kong as a subject, laudable as that may be, in an attempt to fathom the mysteries of its identity. What is both culturally and politically more important is the development of a new Hong Kong subjectivity, that is, a subjectivity constructed not narcissistically but in the very process of negotiating the mutations and permutations of colonialism, nationalism, and capitalism. Anything short of such a subjectivity and all that we will ever find will be predictable variations of discourses on "Western images of Hong Kong this and that," compendia of orientalist kitsch produced by compradorist mentalities. It should be noted, too, that this new subjectivity that we are trying to describe and invent at the same time is not a mere psychologistic category. It is, rather, an affective, political, and social category all at once. It is, I am trying to suggest, a subjectivity that is coaxed into being by the disappearance of old cultural bearings and orientations, which is to say that it is a subjectivity that develops precisely out of a space of disappearance.

Let me turn now to three options, which are really three temptations, that seem to hold out the promise of overcoming the colonial condition, none of which goes far enough: the temptation of the local, the marginal, the cosmopolitan, or what we might call the fallacies of three worldism, two worldism, and one worldism. In each case, some off-the-shelf identity impedes the movement of subjectivity.

It is easy to understand the temptation of the local. Devalued, ignored or subordinated under the hegemonic regimes, the local is now reasserted as a mark of independence. However much one sympathizes with such an attitude (and it is an attitude and not yet a position), there are certain real difficulties involved. One difficulty is related to the fact that the history of colonialism has a hangover effect. What Frantz Fanon and others have analyzed as the psychic mutilations and self-mutilations produced by a colonial episteme do not vanish overnight; a postcolonial subjectivity is not developed without a struggle. For example, the "local" in Hong Kong is not just a matter of adopting Cantonese, the local dialect, instead of English, for the simple reason that the colonialist mentality can find expression in Cantonese just as well as in English. The local is not so easily localized; it is not so much what language we use, as what we use language for. The difficulty with the local, therefore, is in locating it, and this is particularly tricky in a place like Hong Kong with its significant proportion of refugees, migrants, and transients, all of whom could claim local status. Or take the example of architecture: what is local architecture? Is it the Chinese nineteenth-century-style domestic buildings, some of which still exist in the less overbuilt parts of the territory? Or is it the colonial-style monuments like the old Supreme Court building in the Central District, whose preservation is a rare concession to Hong Kong history, that is, history as nostalgia? Or is it also something else that has not yet been perceived and certainly not celebrated as local: the ubiquitous slab-like buildings that represent a local interpretation of the modernist idea of "form follows function" to mean putting up the cheapest, most cost-effective buildings, the minimalism of modernism translated as the maximum in profit margins? What I am suggesting is that the local is *already a translation* (and this is true not only in the last-mentioned case), so that the question of the local cannot be separated from the question of cultural translation itself.

Another temptation for the postcolonial is the lure of the marginal, one version of which is the argument that Jean-François Lyotard makes in *The Postmodern Condition* about little narratives, local knowledge, and paralogies as so many strategies for resisting the master discourses, scientific and legitimated, of the center. In Lyotard's well-known argument, the scientist, operating from the center, questions the "narrative statements" that are on the margins of knowledge and concludes "that they are never subject to argumentation or proof [and hence are not legitimate]. . . . This unequal relationship is an intrinsic effect of the rules specific to each game. We all know its symptoms. It is the entire history of cultural imperialism from the dawn of Western civilization."[11] As this last comment indicates, marginality in Lyotard is the positive link between the postmodern and the postcolonial. As a figure for the self-invention of the postcolonial subject, however, marginality is of doubtful value, an avant-garde romance. First of all, there is a mechanism by which the center can acknowledge and defuse the marginal, namely, by the mechanism of the token. The marginal is acknowledged as a token and so placed and stabilized. Furthermore, the discourse of marginality runs the constant risk of reifying the opposition between margin and center. The marginal then becomes what Jean Baudrillard calls a form of deterrence that reconfirms the center as center, not a form of resistance or a movement elsewhere.[12] Marginality does not necessarily shake up the center or initiate a process of decentering. It merely exercises the center and in so doing strengthens it, by providing a form of political isometrics.

Let me turn now to the model of cosmopolitanism, which for the postcolonial may be the most tempting figure of all. It offers the hope of breaking away from local ghettos and entering the world in full cultural equality. An essay by Ulf Hannerz distinguishes the cosmopolitan from the tourist, the exile, and the expatriate.[13] Hannerz represents cosmopolitanism positively as a state of mind, consisting largely of an interest in and a toleration for otherness, and concludes that such a stance is indispensable at a time of "one world culture." This is a slippery phrase, and we have only to turn to Jorge Luis Borges's classic essay "The Argentine Writer and Tradition" to see both the ambiguity and allure of cosmopolitanism for a postcolonial subject. Borges begins with an ironic argument against localism. He quotes an observation by Edward Gibbon in *The Decline and Fall of the Roman Empire* to the effect that in the Koran, the most Arabian of Arabian books, there are no camels:

> I believe if there were any doubts as to the authenticity of the Koran, this absence of camels would be sufficient to prove it is an Arabian work. It was written by Mohammed, and Mohammed, as an Arab, had no reason to know that camels were especially Arabian; for him they were a part of reality, he had no reason to emphasize them; on the other hand, the first thing a falsifier, a tourist, an Arab nationalist would do is have a surfeit of camels, caravans of camels, on every page.[14]

By contrast, the fallacy of localism is "the idea that Argentine poetry should abound in differential Argentine traits and Argentine local colour."

As an example of poetry representative of Argentine national culture, Borges cites the sonnets in Enrique Banchs's *La Urna*, specifically the lines "the sun shines on the slanting roof / and on the windows. Nightingales / try to say they are in love." Borges points out immediately that in the suburbs of Buenos Aires, the roofs are flat not slanting, while the nightingale is a thoroughly compromised literary image, not a real bird:

> However, I would say that in the use of these conventional images, in these anomalous roofs and nightingales, Argentine architecture and ornithology are of course absent, but we do find in them the Argentine's reticence, his constraint; the fact that Banchs, when speaking of this great suffering, which overwhelms him, when speaking of this woman who has left him and

has left the world empty for him, should have recourse to foreign and conventional images like slanted roofs and nightingales, is significant: significant of Argentine reserve, distrust and reticence, of the difficulty we have in making confessions, in revealing our intimate nature.

Borges scores a point here against simplistic, unmediated notions of the local.

What is dubious, however, is the conclusion that follows: "I believe our tradition is all of Western culture, and I also believe we have a right to this tradition, greater than that which the inhabitants of one or another Western nation might have." In trying to avoid the narrow philistinism of the local, Borges falls into the trap of an optimistic universalism of the cosmopolitan. Is it coincidence that Buenos Aires is also a port city like Hong Kong? In any case, such universalism sees all culture as one in a utopian assertion of equality, but such an assertion tends to ignore or forget the unequal historical conditions of cultural production and reception. What Hannerz puts together in the portmanteau phrase "one world culture" needs separating: world culture (globalism) is not the same as one culture (with its implication that everyone has an equal place).

The ambiguity of the figures of the native, the marginal, and the cosmopolitan as figures of the postcolonial serves to remind us of the problems of representation. In an attempt to appear as a subject in these figures, the postcolonial in fact disappears in these representations and self-representations. This is because these representations of the postcolonial are by now too stable, and a process of immunization has already set in against their power to provoke or to redefine institutional parameters. These representations are now absorbed in the system of signification of the colonial imaginary, and they have no power to shake up that imaginary. Disappearance does not just intentionally wipe out the possibility of postcolonial identity: what is significant is how this wiping out is done. It can wipe out identity precisely by *conferring* plausible identities on the postcolonial—like the native, the marginal, the cosmopolitan. A culture of disappearance gives us identities to take away our subjectivity, emotions to take away our affectivity, a voice to take away representation. However, and this is the interesting point, such a situation can be turned against itself: the wiping out of identity may not be an entirely negative thing, *if it can be taken far enough*. Not all identities are worth preserving. This is to say that disappearance is not only a threat—it is also an opportunity. The moment of asignification when models of identity disappear is also the moment when a postcolonial subject is invented—although the dangers of such a game should not be underestimated. There is one essential condition, however, that must be there if the postcolonial subject is not to be reabsorbed and assimilated: it must not be another stable appearance, another stable identity. It must learn how to survive a culture of disappearance by adopting strategies of disappearance as its own, by giving disappearance itself a different inflection. Making a virtue out of necessity—this could be a working definition of strategy.

The very process of negotiating the mutations and permutations of colonialism, nationalism, and capitalism would require the development of new cultural strategies. Where then can these strategies be found? They will have to be in the new Hong Kong cinema, in certain kinds of writing, in ways of understanding urban space, in theoretically and empirically informed discourses on Hong Kong. This book is not intended to be a survey of Hong Kong culture that tries to include as much as possible; rather, it is intended as a study of Hong Kong culture in a space of disappearance. My subject is a specific cultural space that I hope to evoke through a discussion of cultural forms and practices.

A brief word about method. It is not immediately obvious, even to myself, that every text I have chosen to discuss—whether film, building, or writing—merits close attention. But this is very much the nature of the enterprise, that in the space I am evoking the distinction between the meritorious and the meretricious is frequently indiscernible. Very often, I can develop the hints of what I find to be fascinating in my chosen texts only by first bracketing the question of merit. Nevertheless, we should remember that it was precisely by setting aside the question of merit that Sigfried Kracauer and Walter Benjamin were able to develop the crucial concept of *distraction* as a means of opening up to analysis the problematic cultural space of their own time.[15] In their hands, distraction was not an idealization of absent-mindedness, but a strategy of perception in a rapidly changing cultural situation that threatened to outpace critical understanding of a more orthodox kind. The strategy allowed them to change the objects of attention and to attend to the trivial and the superficial as signifiers of culture as well. It is in this spirit but with necessarily different methods that I will be trying to read the Hong Kong cultural texts. Both their perfections and imperfections may tell us something more about the elusiveness of colonial space as a space of disappearance than "theories of colonialism" developed under different sociopolitical circumstances.

2

The New Hong Kong Cinema and the *Déjà Disparu*

The Déjà Disparu

According to Gilles Deleuze, the various European cinemas became "modern" at different times, but always at the moment when they had to come up with new cinematic images in response to new historical situations: "The timing is something like: around 1948, Italy; about 1958, France; about 1968, Germany."[1] We might now arguably add, going beyond Europe, about 1982, Hong Kong, which was the year of Margaret Thatcher's visit to China. Since that date, it has become increasingly apparent that a new Hong Kong cinema has been emerging. It is both a popular cinema and a cinema of auteurs, with names like Ann Hui, Tsui Hark, Allen Fong, John Woo, Stanley Kwan, and Wong Kar-wai gaining not only local acclaim but also a certain measure of international recognition. Contrary to a widespread impression, however, this new cinema is not essentially a cinema of action or a "cinema of blazing passions," which was how one popular festival of Hong Kong films was billed in the United States. What is interesting is that it is a cinema that responds to a specific and unprecedented historical situation, what I have called a space of disappearance where "imperialism" and "globalism" are imbricated with each other. History now goes through strange loops and becomes difficult to represent in terms of traditional realism. If real history is becoming more incredible by the day, we will have to resort to the incredible to keep up with it.

Hence the frequent excesses and exaggerations of the new Hong Kong cinema: they register a sense of the incredible as real, somewhat as in Jorge Luis Borges's story *Emma Zunz*. Certain of the justice of her vengeance, Emma Zunz commits a murder and presents it as self-defense by telling an incredible story: "Actually, the story *was* incredible, but it impressed everyone because substantially it was true. True was Emma Zunz's tone, true was her shame, true was her hate. True also was the outrage she had suffered: only the circumstances were false, the time and one or two proper names."[2] In Borges's story, it is not so much that the end justifies the means, but, rather, that ends and means have become disconnected, in a time that is out of joint. Hence other kinds of connections have to be made. Such dislocations and novel connections also typify the new Hong Kong cinema and the images we find in them.

This allows us to see why cinema has such a privileged position in Hong Kong's culture of disappearance, quite apart from the fact that it is the most developed and popular of Hong Kong's cultural forms. It is in the images of the new cinema that the history of contemporary Hong Kong with all its anxieties and contradictions can be read. However, the response to this new cinema, even by well-informed local and foreign critics, is largely misleading, suggesting that the question of its evaluation is far from simple. In fact, on the evidence of what has been written about it, the more interesting examples of recent Hong Kong cinema must be among the most elusive films being made today.

Most critical opinion on Hong Kong films seems divided between criticizing it for its relentless commercialism or applauding it for (what is perceived as) its high camp qualities: neither view is very instructive. For example, Paul Fonoroff, a Hong Kong-based student of local film history can ask about films currently being made, "What makes Hong Kong films so mediocre?"[3] and suggest commercialism, low audience expectations, the lack of imaginative producers as answers. The respected local film critic Li Cheuk-to, in a review of films made in 1988–89, also points to the relentless commercial pressures exerted by film producers and distributors that leave Hong Kong directors little room for artistic maneuvering. He concludes his review by noting that "the defects of the system and the lack of creative talent form the greatest obstacles and sources of worry that hamper the emergence of an artistically excellent Hong Kong cinema."[4] Other critics go on to link commercialism to a certain filmic "style" that is associated with the Hong Kong cinema. "Welcome to the new wave of Hong

Kong cinema," writes Jeffrey Ressner in the *New York Times*—"films characterized by comic-book images, hyperkinetic quick cuts and mind-boggling
story lines. . . . Unlike American films, Hong Kong movies are produced in
assembly-line fashion."[5] And even in many ways an astute and thoughtful
essay by Geoffrey O'Brien (in the *New York Review of Books*) cannot finally
resist taking up the refrain about commercialism: "It is one of the ironies
of the situation that the dangers of 1997 can make a frankly commercial,
assembly-line cinema—dedicated to nothing more uplifting than the fleeting pleasures of spectacle and narration—look somewhat like an endan-
gered ecosystem."[6]

On the other hand, when the Hong Kong cinema is praised (interestingly enough, more often by foreign than by local critics), it is for its action sequences, its slick editing, its mastery of special effects that would
"make even George Lucas envious" (Ressner), as if the mere downplaying
of dialogue, narrative structure, or even intelligence somehow made Hong
Kong cinema more immediate, more like "pure cinema," more akin to the
work of Buster Keaton or the Keystone Cops. It is thus that the Hong
Kong cinema is elevated from commercial trash status to cult art status by
way of the axiological reversals of camp. O'Brien writes, with more than a
hint of lyricism, about the kung fu movie:

> In the best examples of the genre . . . the grace and flexibility of the per-
> formers—augmented by razor-fast editing, slow-motion trampoline leaps,
> and the guttural and percussive punctuations of the soundtrack—created
> unmediated cinematic pleasure. The movie did not represent anything at
> all; it presented. . . . the Hong Kong cinema retains an athleticism which
> Hollywood, with a few fleeting exceptions, lost after the era of Douglas
> Fairbanks and Buster Keaton.

In other words, a film should not mean but be, and in a backhanded kind of
way, Hong Kong films are seen to satisfy this requirement very well. To
praise the Hong Kong cinema in these terms is not only to prize it loose of
its very specific cultural space; it is also to place the kung fu films of Bruce
Lee and Jackie Chan, and more recently the gangster epics of John Woo
and his imitators, at the center of Hong Kong's film history, and to present
them as the examples par excellence of an emergent international Hong
Kong cinema. The question is whether such an evaluation is either justi-
fied or perceptive enough.

The problem with putting the whole emphasis on commercialism and
the campiness of the action movie is that Hong Kong cinema tends to be
too easily homogenized as a result. It is true that the films of Bruce Lee, Jackie

Chan, and John Woo have had the most international exposure and are therefore the best-known Hong Kong films abroad. Of the trio, it is John Woo who has succeeded in exporting his idea of the action film to Hollywood; his latest films (*Hard Boiled*, 1992; *Hard Target*, 1993) were produced there. But all these action films—which are undeniably important for the Hong Kong film industry and which, it must be said, have their own interest—represent only one side of the new Hong Kong cinema. Even if we agree with O'Brien that "Hong Kong at present makes the most raucous and least contemplative films on the planet," it also makes other kinds of films as well. There is, in other words, no easy homogeneity to Hong Kong cinema, in spite of appearances. It is a gross simplification to say, as O'Brien does, that "taken together, Hong Kong movies . . . constitute a single metanarrative, incorporating every available variant of sentimental, melodramatic and horrific plotting, set to the beat of non-stop synthesized pop music." How, we might ask, could such a cinema of mindless pleasures command any but the most superficial kind of international attention or merit anything more than a casual sociological study? What makes the Hong Kong cinema an international cinema will have to be sought elsewhere, especially if we realize that it is a cinema that can now accommodate the stylish baroque obsessions of a Stanley Kwan, the visual and cognitive ambivalences of a Wong Kar-wai, the dismantlings of nostalgia of an Ann Hui, the reworkings of traditional storytelling of a Tsui Hark. The films that are made cannot be reduced to "a single metanarrative" but represent so many disparate attempts to evoke a problematic cultural space. And it is ultimately by attending to the relationship of Hong Kong cinema to this cultural space that we will arrive at a different account of Hong Kong cinema and its history.

To address the nature of Hong Kong's cultural space as it relates to cinema, we must again raise the question of commercialism, but in a different way. We need to reexamine the assumption that strong commercial pressures can result only in poorly made films, by questioning the old paradigm that constructs an absolute opposition between "commercialism" and "art." The terms of this opposition are extremely unstable in any case, as indeed the history of cinema itself can testify. Cinema was never art in any docile sense; on the contrary, it has always challenged accepted notions of art. But this lesson is always one that has to be learned anew because the old paradigm can resurface in a different guise, as in the distinction between a mainstream commercial cinema and an alternative art cinema.

As far as the Hong Kong cinema is concerned, the notion of the art film is more a liability than an asset. It would be much better, therefore, to begin by saying that the innovative Hong Kong cinema is not primarily directed at establishing itself as an alternative or art cinema, and to draw out the implications of this statement. With few exceptions, films made in Hong Kong are all part of the mainstream; all make use, to the full extent that their budgets allow, of established stars, established genres, and spectacle. To speak of "new wave" directors or "alternative" cinema in this situation is misleading, especially if one's idea of the new wave is Jean-Luc Godard or Alain Resnais. However—and this is the crucial point—such a state of affairs is not as limiting as it sounds because there are different ways of being part of the mainstream. If commercialism is indeed a necessary given that turns films into commodities, it is still possible, as Walter Benjamin said of Charles Baudelaire, to elicit the aura proper to the commodity—that is to say, to explore the cultural possibilities of what looks like a negative situation.[7] Such an enterprise may require the invention of new kinds of filmmaking strategies other than, say, the direct subversions of mainstream film practices that we see in Godard and Resnais. These new strategies should be the focus of our critical attention, and I shall be turning to them later when I discuss individual films. The point at the moment is that the use of mainstream forms in Hong Kong cinema is not *necessarily* a sign of intellectual inertia or of pandering to the masses. It is more a sign of the slippery nature of Hong Kong's cultural space.

The ambiguity of the commercial in Hong Kong cinema can be clarified to some extent by a comparison with the new Chinese cinema on the mainland. The early films of Chen Kaige, Zhang Yimou, Tian Zhuangzhuang, Huang Jianxiu , and so on—the so-called Fifth Generation—are quite militantly noncommercial compared to their Hong Kong counterparts, with few compromises made to please an audience. There are many reasons for this, but one major reason is that while economics has always been a factor in film production, it was less decisive in the case of the Fifth Generation insofar as the Chinese system of film production and distribution in the early- and mid-eighties amounted almost to a form of state subsidy. This meant that the Fifth Generation could reinvent modernism, explore the possibilities of the spare image, experiment with nonlinear narration, and so on, without having to worry too much about any but an ideal audience. Their "sharply defined pictures devoid of any didactic purpose, surrounded by silence and open to multiple interpretations" that so impressed O'Brien and that he contrasts to the noisiness of the Hong Kong cinema were made possible at least partly by state support.

The new Chinese cinema, however, presents a paradox of its own, one that George S. Semsel captures well when he notes with some surprise that "what my American colleagues and I failed to acknowledge was that the films we celebrated as signs of a Chinese 'new wave' had been produced within the dominant studio system of China, that those who made them did not represent an alternative, independent cinema."[8] He goes on to speak of other filmmakers who tried to work independently of the state and hence had to fall back on market support. Although Semsel puts his point a little too baldly, he does make the valid suggestion that independence could mean different things: freedom from the market or freedom from state support, that is, that independence, too, could be as ambiguous as commercialism. Significantly, when the situation changed dramatically after the 1989 Tiananmen Massacre when state funding for films dried up and Chinese directors had to look to Hong Kong and Taiwan for financial backing, so, too, did the film aesthetics of the Fifth Generation change to some extent. *Yellow Earth* (1984) and *Red Sorghum* (1987) are very different from *Raise the Red Lantern* (1991) and *Farewell My Concubine* (1994). The second pair of films, in their use of spectacle, big-name stars, and familiar forms of narrative appropriate the devices of the commercial film, but not entirely to their own detriment. It was ironically *Farewell My Concubine*, Chen Kaige's "commercial" film, that finally won him the major international film award that had eluded him for so long.

Unlike the Chinese cinema, the Hong Kong cinema cannot rely on any form of subsidy. It cannot therefore reject commercialism, which is the sine qua non of its existence. The Hong Kong cinema has to be popular in order to be at all. The effective strategy consists not of finding alternatives to the system, but alternatives within the system. The commercial is not necessarily the junkyard of cinema, just as the noncommercial is not necessarily the guarantee of quality or even of integrity. In any case, a certain impurity in the form of an ambiguity toward commercialism is the rule in Hong Kong cinema. But it is an impurity that can yield positive results, as a number of outstanding Hong Kong films made recently show, insofar as it goes together with an awareness that good films are not made according to one immutable set of rules.

In relation to commercialism, the isolated case of Allen Fong, who is very much the exception that proves the rule, becomes highly interesting. His noncommercial work seems to me to be a failure of a particularly valuable and significant kind. Take his best-known film *Father and Son* (1981), which is a semiautobiographical story about growing up in Hong Kong's crowded housing estates. It is a film shot in a kind of neorealist documentary style, which eschews the use of big-name stars and spectacular effects.

The film shows us another side of Hong Kong, not the sensational world of rapacious consumption and high-tech information but the everyday world of common people. *Father and Son* has all the uncompromising integrity of the early work of the Fifth Generation, even without the benefit of state subsidy. Fong does not make use of currently popular film genres and is relatively unconcerned about packaging, publicity, and distribution. Not surprisingly, he finds it particularly difficult to get funding for his projects. He wryly describes himself and like-minded filmmakers as "magicians on how to survive."[9] Fong has introduced a note of honesty and sincerity to Hong Kong cinema. For reasons that will be obvious in a moment, however, his straightforward neorealist style of filmmaking seems incapable of addressing the historical paradoxes of contemporary Hong Kong and the problematics of disappearance. *Father and Son* is set almost exclusively in the past, showing in one long flashback a Hong Kong that has almost completely vanished with the advent of air travel. The film is bracketed significantly by shots of an airplane landing and taking off. When Ann Hui uses flashback, it will not be to suggest the stability of the past, and when Stanley Kwan uses the documentary style, it will not imply a faith in the ability of "the real" to speak and be heard. For better or for worse, it has been left to other directors less wary of the dangers of working within the system to make the decisively important films of the new Hong Kong cinema.

We turn now to the question of disappearance. It is not enough to think about Hong Kong cinema simply in terms of a tight commercial space occasionally opened up by individual talent, on the model of auteurs in Hollywood. The situation is both more interesting and more complicated, brought about by the social and political transformations that took place in the early eighties when it became clear that Hong Kong would revert to Chinese rule in July 1997. These transformations have produced an open-ended situation that is still in the process of definition—who knows what will happen to Hong Kong after 1997? Nevertheless, in relation to cinema, a number of changes are already discernible, like a new kind of filmmaker, an urgent new subject matter, and changes both in the nature of the audience and in the conditions of viewing. July 1997 is not just a terminal date that falls sometime in the future. It is, all at once, an ever-present irritant, a provocation, and a catalyst for change. It turns Hong Kong into what Paul Virilio calls a "hyper-anticipatory and predictive" society, where time is experienced very much in the future perfect tense.[10]

The emergence of the new Hong Kong cinema could be dated to the early eighties because, while on one level the Hong Kong film industry just went on doing what it had been doing with relative financial success, on another level the eighties saw decisive changes that would turn Hong Kong cinema into something qualitatively different from what went before. This is not to dismiss the earlier cinema, but simply to affirm that the new cinema has to be judged by different rules. In the first place, the early eighties was the moment when a new generation of Hong Kong-born filmmakers, educated in film schools abroad and with no direct ties to either China or Taiwan, turned to filmmaking after a period of apprenticeship in local television. The result was a cinema that in terms of technical competence and thematic richness represented a qualitative leap forward. Three films released in 1982 can be taken to exemplify this moment: Tsui Hark's *Zu: Warriors from the Magic Mountain*, a kung fu film distinguished by its brilliant mastery of special effects; Ann Hui's *Boat People*, about Vietnamese refugees, where cinema is used to deal with pressing social and political issues; and Patrick Tam's *Nomad*, about disaffected youths in urban Hong Kong. But 1982 was also the year of Margaret Thatcher's visit to China, which began a process of negotiation that culminated in the Joint Declaration of 1984 returning Hong Kong to China in 1997. The Joint Declaration caused a certain amount of anxiety, even though one of its terms is that the sociopolitical structure of Hong Kong will remain unchanged for fifty years (according to the slogan "One country, two systems"). But it also had another effect: it made Hong Kong people look at the place with new eyes. It is as if the possibility of such a social and cultural space disappearing, in the form we know it today, has led to our seeing it in all its complexity and contradiction for the first time, an instance, as Benjamin would have said, of love at last sight. The consequences for cinema are considerable. The Hong Kong cinema, even while it remains a popular commercial cinema, now addresses a public in the process of changing—a public suddenly anxious about its cultural identity because so many issues of social and political liberties hinge on that question. It would be that much harder for Hong Kong citizens to argue the case for political autonomy after 1997 if it could not make the case for cultural identity now. This might allow us to try out the following initial formulation: the new Hong Kong cinema deserves attention because it has finally found a worthy subject— it has found Hong Kong itself as a subject. Is it possible, then, to say about the new Hong Kong cinema that its real emergence could be dated not to the moment when Bruce Lee punched and kicked his way to international stardom, or to the moment when it caught up in terms of technical competence and sophistication with the rest of the world, but to the moment when it could take Hong Kong itself as its privileged subject of interest and inquiry?

Such a generalization would be tempting to make, but it could not be made without some very careful qualifications. It is not the *appearance* of new themes or new subject matter that is significant, for example, like reiterations of the question of Hong Kong's cultural identity or anxiety over 1997. Once these themes begin to appear, they tend to get repeated ad nauseum, very much like gossip. Almost every film made since the mideighties, regardless of quality or seriousness of intention, seems constrained to make some mandatory reference to 1997. For example, it is an issue that dominates Evans Chan's *To Liv(e)* (1990), a film that takes itself very seriously indeed, about the international response to Hong Kong's treatment of the Vietnamese boat people. The pun in the title alludes to Liv Ullmann, the celebrated star of Ingmar Bergman films turned human-rights campaigner, to whom the protagonist writes agonized letters. But 1997 is just as important a reference in Tsui Hark's shameless potboiler *Wicked City* (1992), a *Bladerunner* rip-off about reptilian humanoids plotting to take over the city on that fatal date. Similarly, many gangster films from *A Better Tomorrow* to Johnny Mak's *Long Arm of the Law* can be read as allegories of 1997. It is not the appearance of "Hong Kong themes," then, that is significant in the new Hong Kong cinema, but, rather, what I call a problematic of disappearance: that is to say, a sense of the elusiveness, the slipperiness, the ambivalences of Hong Kong's cultural space that some Hong Kong filmmakers have caught in their use of the film medium, in their explorations of history and memory, in their excavation of the evocative detail—*regardless of subject matter*. More often than not, these films do not even make any direct reference to Hong Kong's political situation today, and they cover a wide spectrum of popular genres. Nevertheless, as films they are both products and analyses of a cultural space of disappearance, as well as responses to it. A short list would include Wong Kar-wai's first four films; Ann Hui's *Song of the Exile;* Stanley Kwan's *Rouge* and *Center Stage;* and Tsui Hark's *Once upon a Time in China* series. It is the representation of disappearances in new cinematic images that is crucial for the Hong Kong cinema.

One way of explaining the problematic of disappearance is by considering the current interest in Hong Kong by Hong Kong people themselves. This is in some strange way a new phenomenon that requires some comment. There has of course always been widespread interest in Hong Kong on the part of locals and foreigners alike, especially since 1949 when the city embarked in earnest on its spectacular international career. The economist Milton Friedman, we remember, once put Hong Kong forward as the model of a capitalist utopia. But until recently this interest was focused primarily on economics and politics, and to a lesser extent (attributable perhaps to colonialist embarrassment) on history. From these kinds of perspectives, many studies of Hong Kong are available. However, when it came to the much more elusive question of Hong Kong culture, all we found was largely mystification and disavowal. To avoid the issue of Hong Kong culture, locals and expatriates alike used to take refuge behind the ideological image of Hong Kong as a "cultural desert," as if culture meant only Shakespeare, Beethoven, and the like, or even Peking Opera for that matter, the scarcity of all of which was loudly bemoaned. On the question of culture, it was as if the Hong Kong person lived through a version of what Sigmund Freud called the "family romance": the fantasy that some children have that their real parents are not their actual parents. The result is that stories about Hong Kong always turned into stories about somewhere else, as if Hong Kong culture were somehow not a subject. This is a case of what Freud calls "negative hallucination": to reiterate a point I made in chapter 1, if hallucination is seeing what is not there, then reverse hallucination is not seeing what is there.

This reverse hallucination requires us to qualify a little our initial formulation about Hong Kong cinema: it may have found a subject, Hong Kong itself, but Hong Kong as a subject is one that threatens to get easily lost again. This time around the threat will not be that there is no interest in Hong Kong—Hong Kong is today very much on the agenda. The threat will be that Hong Kong as a subject will be presented and represented in terms of some of the old *binarisms* whose function it is to restabilize differences and domesticate change, for example, binarisms like East and West, or tradition and modernity. In other words, the danger now is that Hong Kong will disappear as a subject, *not by being ignored but by being represented in the good old ways.* Precisely because Hong Kong is such an elusive subject, there is a temptation to use, and to believe in, the available forms of representation and misrepresentation. This is *dis-appearance* in a very specific sense (imagine the term as hyphenated), in that it gives us a reality that is not so much hidden as purloined, a reality that is overlooked because it is looked at in the old familiar ways. Furthermore, the binarisms used to represent Hong Kong as a subject give us not so much a sense of déjà vu, as the even more uncanny feeling of what we might call the *déjà disparu*: the feeling that what is new and unique about the situation is always already gone, and we are left holding a handful of clichés, or a cluster of memories of what has never been. It is as if the speed of current events is producing a radical desynchronization: the generation of more and more images to the point of visual saturation going together with a general regression of viewing, an inability to read what is given to view—in other words, the state of reverse hallucination.

There is an important relation, then, between the new Hong Kong cinema and the *déjà disparu*: its main task is to find means of outflanking, or simply keeping pace with, a subject always on the point of disappearing—in other words, its task is to construct images out of clichés. Some examples might be Stanley Kwan's drawing on the uncanniness of the ghost story in *Rouge*, or Wong Kar-wai's representations of violent actions that do not quite resolve themselves into clear images in *As Tears Go By*, or Ann Hui's *mise-en-abîme* of memory in *Song of the Exile*. These are some of the films of the new Hong Kong cinema that define for us the spatial conditions of viewing and of filmmaking, where the act of looking itself has become problematic: the more you try to make the world hold still in a reflective gaze, the more it moves under you. These films do not so much thematize Hong Kong culture as they give us a critical experience of Hong Kong's cultural space by problematizing the viewing process. This may also explain why so many of the innovative films are situated in a space between "fact" and "fiction," allowing the specular, the given-to-be-seen, to retain a certain critical speculative edge.

The ambiguity of commercialism and the paradoxes of disappearance can now be related to five features of the new Hong Kong cinema, the first of which involves the question of history and its spatialization. As a city, Hong Kong has been very much the plaything and ambiguous beneficiary of history. Colonized by the British in the nineteenth century; occupied by the Japanese in the second World War; swelled by the influx of refugees from communist China after 1949, which gave it so many of its cooks and tailors and entrepreneurs; taken in hand by the multinationals as it developed into an international city; and now to be returned to China—Hong Kong's history is one of shock and radical changes. As if to protect themselves against this series of traumas, Hong Kong people have little memory and no sentiment for the past. The general attitude to everything, sometimes indistinguishable from the spirit of enterprise, is cancel out and pass on. But history exists, if not in surviving monuments or written records, then in the jostling anachronisms and spatial juxtapositions that are seen on every street; that is, history is inscribed in spatial relations. When the Hong Kong Shanghai Bank building designed by Norman Foster was being built, for example, this ultra-high-tech multinational building was surrounded by traditional Chinese bamboo scaffolding: an image of history as palimpsest. One of the features of new Hong Kong cinema is its sensitivity to spatial issues, in other words, to dislocations and discontinuities, and its adoption of spatial narratives both to underline and to come to terms with these historical anachronisms and achronisms: space as a means of reading the elusiveness of history. We get a better sense of the history of Hong Kong through its new cinema (and architecture) than is currently available in any history book.

Related to the question of space is that of affectivity. In a dislocated space, affectivity in turn becomes problematic. It is as if all the ways of relating have somehow shifted, the bonds that join us to others as friends and lovers, as daughters and sons blurring like the lines on a television screen that is not tracking properly. It is not just a question of traditional emotional responses versus modern indifference: the opposition between tradition and modernity is already too stable and predictable. Rather, what we find represented now are emotions that do not belong to anybody or to any situation—affective intensities with no name. Thus in Stanley Kwan's *Love unto Waste* (1986), a kind of Felliniesque study of decadence, love is a bad habit or a whim or a weakness, an expense of spirit in a waste of shame, a theme he explores again in the more recent *Red Rose, White Rose* (1994). In *Rouge* the most intense emotion belongs to a ghost. In Wong Kar-wai's *Days of Being Wild* (1991), with its structure of interlapping stories, human relations may still be painful, but they have lost all their *serious* aspects and take on instead a *serial* quality of transferences, exchanges, and repetitions—all to the background music of old dance-hall songs with their suggestions of faded passions.

From what vantage point can the filmmaker describe this cultural space and sick eros? Certainly not from the outside, from a privileged critical distance. So while there are a number of successful comedies, there are no parodies or ironic presentations of Hong Kong society in the new Hong Kong cinema comparable to, say, Robert Altman's ironic portraits of America in *Nashville* (1975) or *A Wedding* (1978). The position of the Hong Kong filmmaker, then, is what we might call a position of critical proximity, where one is always a part of what one is criticizing. This brings me to a third observation about the new Hong Kong cinema, which concerns the use of genres. Given commercial pressures, it is understandable that even the most independent of filmmakers find themselves working with popular genres like the gangster (or "hero") film, the ghost story, and the kung fu movie. What is remarkable, however, is that these filmmakers produce some of their best work within these genres (this is an example of what I mean by critical proximity). Although many Hong Kong films are meretricious and formulaic, we also find Wong Kar-wai's *As Tears Go By* (a gangster film), Stanley Kwan's *Rouge* (a ghost film), and Tsui Hark's *Once upon a Time in China: Part I* (a kung fu movie). By no means parodies of their respective genres, these films use the limits of genre as a discipline and a challenge.

Fourth, the language of the new Hong Kong cinema is Cantonese (or more precisely, that version of Cantonese practiced in Hong Kong). This was not always the case. In the late seventies the sociologist I. C. Jarvie divided Hong Kong film into Cantonese and Mandarin, arguing that Cantonese movies were un-Westernized and designed entirely for local consumption, while Mandarin movies were cosmopolitan, technically accomplished, and in touch with the contemporary world.[11] If these observations had some cogency for the early seventies, they have proved to be irrelevant for Hong Kong cinema in the eighties and nineties. The new Hong Kong cinema has indeed gone over to Cantonese, as has pop music (what is called Canto-rock). But in doing so, it has not simply asserted the importance of the local; it has also changed the way in which the local is regarded. In the older Cantonese movies, the local was an ethos of exclusion: it defined a narrow homogeneous social space where foreigners and foreign elements had no place, which is what gives these old movies, when we watch them now, a certain campy quality. The new localism, on the other hand, investigates the dislocations of the local, where the local is something unstable that mutates right in front of our eyes, like the language itself. Hong Kong Cantonese now is sprinkled with snatches of Mandarin, English, and barbarous sounding words and phrases—a hybrid language coming out of a hybrid space. It is by being local in this way that the new Hong Kong cinema is most international. Conversely, some of the attempts to be international—by using a foreign city as background, for example, as in Clara Law's well-regarded *Autumn Story*, a film about Hong Kong Chinese in New York made in the late eighties—may strike us as awkward and provincial.

Finally, the new localism does not just present Hong Kong as a subject worthy of attention; it develops what we might call a new Hong Kong subjectivity as it moves toward a difficult and idiosyncratic form of postcoloniality. The fifth feature of the new Hong Kong cinema is the presence of a politics of identity, but it is a politics that expresses itself best when expressed indirectly, for example, in the introduction of new kinds of cinematic images or in the rewriting of film genres. We will come back to the question of images and other features of the Hong Kong cinema when we look at individual films, but this may be the place to say a word

about the politics of the kung fu genre, about kung fu as an indirect representation of the changing nature of coloniality in Hong Kong.

The kung fu/martial arts genre, from Bruce Lee's *The Big Boss* (1971)
through the offerings of Jackie Chan and Tsui Hark, to Wong Kar-wai's
recent *Ashes of Time* (1994), has gone through a number of distinct transformations, each one a rewriting of the genre. Such films are not expected
to do much more than provide entertainment through visual spectacle
(which is one reason why the brilliant and long-awaited *Ashes of Time* was
such a disappointment to local audiences); but perhaps exactly because of
that, we see all the more clearly the unstable shape of coloniality inscribed
in these films over a period of roughly twenty-five years, undoubtedly the
most important years in Hong Kong's short history. It is not that the kung
fu film is ever a direct critique of colonialism; rather, that the ethos of
(mainly) male heroism and personal prowess so central to the genre has
to define itself in relation to *what is felt to be possible* in a changing colonial
situation. In defining heroism, it defines by implication the colonial situation itself.

Bruce Lee was a child star in the local Cantonese cinema, and he learned
his kung fu in Hong Kong. In the United States, he became a martial arts
instructor who taught kung fu to Hollywood stars and got a minor and
ethnically stereotyped part in the television series *The Green Hornet*. He was
passed over for the role of Kane in the successful series *Kung Fu* that went
to David Carradine. However, when he returned to Hong Kong in the
early seventies at the beginning of the local craze for better-quality martial
arts films, which came in the wake of the international success of Akira
Kurosawa's sword-play epics *Sanjuro* and *Yojimbo*, things were very different. He returned with the cachet of foreignness: the repatriate was an expatriate. And he returned with impeccable martial arts credentials, having
won a number of international martial arts competitions. His first film, *The
Big Boss*, set the pattern. Here was an actor who could really kick and
punch, and it introduced a new level of authenticity and a new type of
hero to the Hong Kong cinema, what Geoffrey O'Brien calls the stuntman
as hero. But there was another equally important element in Lee's series of
films, whether directed by him or others. The physical authenticity was
keyed to something else, something much more elusive, namely, the
reassertion of an authentic and heroic Chinese identity. The repatriate/
expatriate was also a patriot, the patriotism expressing itself as a form of
anticolonialism. There was a strong xenophobic tone in the Lee films,
which took the form of the Chinese hero beating up Japanese or Cau-

casians in beautifully choreographed action sequences. The anticolonialism was slightly forced, however, and cannot be taken too literally. It came at the moment when both Bruce Lee and Hong Kong began to embark on very successful international careers. Hence two features can be noted. First, the anticolonial anger did not refer to very much in the present, but only to *memories* of slights and insults suffered in the past: memories belonging to another place and to an older generation. It was as if Bruce Lee were fighting again in a new Boxer Rebellion through the medium of cinema, in much the same way that Hollywood refought the Vietnam War. The second feature was the vaguely directed animus and the stereotyped opponents, as if there were no idea who the "enemy" really was. Every time Lee fights, he seems to fall into a trance and acts like someone shadow-boxing. As a result the films kick and punch themselves into a corner. *Fist of Fury* (1972) ends emblematically with Lee caught in a freeze-frame executing a high kick, leaving both its star and all the plot strands up in the air.

Jackie Chan marks a second moment in the development of the martial arts genre, and a different moment in colonial history. With Lee's death, a successor had to be found. Like Lee, Chan is a martial arts expert, and he makes it a point of honor to perform all the action stunts himself. One of Jackie Chan's first films is called in fact *New Fist of Fury* (1976) to underline the succession. But while villainous colonizers are still around, everything now has a touch of slapstick. The result is essentially a transformation of the genre into kung fu comedy. The Jackie Chan character created in *Drunken Master* (1978) is neither a patriot nor an expatriate; he is just a regular local boy with good but not invincible skills. The heroism is not to be taken too seriously. Jackie Chan has the good humor of the professional rather than the dark taciturnity of Bruce Lee's avenging angel. The good humor is significant because it could be related very closely to the relaxation of colonial tensions in Hong Kong so noticeable in the late seventies, a mood that lasted until Thatcher's visit to China in 1982. This was a moment when signs for optimism, like the end of the Chinese Cultural Revolution, were everywhere, and colonialism seemed almost an irrelevance, no more than a formal administrative presence that did not interfere with the real life of the colony. A new sense of how it was local ingenuity and professionalism more than imported talent that had brought about the city's great success came with the force of a revelation. In other words, it was a growing confidence in Hong Kong's international viability that led to a rediscovery of the local, just as it was Bruce Lee who prepared the way for Jackie Chan. Nor is it accidental that Jackie Chan's kung fu comedy coincided with the new brand of comedy introduced by the Hui brothers, Michael and Sam, who used current Cantonese slang to explore the peculiarities of the local situation, often to brilliant effect. It was also during this period that Sam Hui introduced what has since been known as Canto-pop, where the lyrics are in the local idiom rather than in English or Mandarin. The new "local" culture was nonprovincial and exciting, and it appealed to a wide audience, unlike the earlier localism that appealed mainly to the non-Anglophone sectors of the community. All these developments changed the way Hong Kong people looked at local culture and, for a while, at colonialism—that is to say, until the eighties, which experienced the double trauma of the Sino-British Joint Declaration and the Tiananmen Massacre. Significantly, in the eighties the kung fu genre, too, fell into decline, only to reemerge in the nineties in two different forms in films by Tsui Hark and Wong Kar-wai. It is in the style of these new kung fu films that we sense that some radical changes in the nature of coloniality in Hong Kong have indeed taken place.

In these kung fu films of the nineties, two realizations have sunk in. First, it is no longer possible to appeal with any conviction to some vague notion of Chineseness, as China itself may turn out to be the future colonizer, in fact if not in name, once the present one has departed. Second, it is no longer possible to see local developments as separable or proceeding in isolation from global developments. It is from this perspective that we can interestingly consider the kung fu films of Tsui Hark, which obliquely convey the message that colonialism is on the point of becoming obsolete. This is particularly clear in the series *Once upon a Time in China*, the first of which appeared in 1991. The series deals with stories about the legendary Chinese master, Wong Fei Hung, and there are many action sequences and references to history and colonial history. At one point, Sun Yat-sen makes an appearance, reminiscent of the way historical figures keep appearing in *Forrest Gump*. This comparison with *Gump* suggests that what sets the series apart are not the authenticities of action or history but its mastery of *special effects*. In Tsui Hark's films, it is no longer stuntmen but special effects that are the real heroes. Tsui Hark's star Jet Li (who interestingly enough is mainland Chinese) knows his kung fu, but there are no more authentic stars/heroes of the order of Bruce Lee, as the real is more and more being "coproduced" through special effects. For example, in the marvelous fight between Wong Fei Hung and another kung fu master that climaxes the first *Once upon a Time in China*, Tsui Hark makes the two characters do wonderful gravity-defying things with ladders, but our main interest is focused on how Tsui Hark *films* these sequences rather than on the athleticism of the actors. This interest in special effects implies not only that the Hong

Kong cinema has caught up with the new technologies; more important, it now places the filmic action in a new technological and, by implication, transnational space where (we might be tempted to believe in an optimistic moment) the problem of colonialism will have been a thing of the past. Tsui Hark's kung fu series may be set in the past, but it is a past reproduced by laser.

Another view of technology and colonialism can be read in Wong Kar-wai's *Ashes of Time* (1994), one of the most remarkable films to have come out of the new Hong Kong cinema. It is Wong's version of the martial arts epic, made almost contemporaneously with Tsui Hark's kung fu films, but the style and emphases are very different. The beautiful cinematography of Chris Doyle merely serves to emphasize the film's somber tone, its focus on a landscape of ruins. As we watch the characters in their Issey Miyake-like costumes parade across desert and swamp in a series of fascinating tableaux, it is like watching a pavane. There is not one but four heroes, and the film uses a number of spectacular special effects; but it soon becomes clear that both heroism and special effects, as well as visuality itself, are being reexamined and found wanting. Consider the fight sequence that opens the film, involving the story's main figure Ouyang Feng. It is no longer a choreography of human bodies in motion that we see. In fact, we do not know what it is we are seeing. Things have now been speeded up to such an extent that what we find is only a composition of light and color in which all action has dissolved—a kind of abstract expressionism or action painting. It is not possible, therefore, to discern who is doing what to whom. The heroic space of Bruce Lee is now a *blind space* (one of the four heroes in fact is going blind); moreover, it is a blind space that comes from an *excess* of light and movement, that is to say, an excess of Tsui Hark-style special effects. *Ashes of Time* gives us a kind of double dystopia, where heroism loses its raison d'être and special effects lose their air of optimism and exhilaration. Wong's film marks a point of *degeneration* of the genre, the moment when the genre self-destructs. The idea of presence and authenticity implied in the ethos of heroism is subverted, and the hope of happy inscription in a technology-based global utopia implied in the optimistic use of special effects is imploded. In this indirect way the film speaks to some of the problems and anxieties of *technocolonialism*, which *shows* itself only abstractly and negatively as something that cannot be directly represented, particularly not by means of sophisticated technological equipment. As for the Hong Kong kung fu film as a whole, it suggests that colonialism itself is made up of a series of slippery dislocations: a kind of *morphing*.

Some Representative Films of the New Hong Kong Cinema

The four films I have chosen as representative of the new Hong Kong cinema are Wong Kar-wai's debut film *As Tears Go By* (1988) (we will be looking at Wong's other films in the next chapter); Ann Hui's domestic melodrama *Song of the Exile* (1990); Stanley Kwan's ghost film *Rouge* (1988); and his "bio-pic" *Center Stage* (1991). While these four films are very different from each other, what they do have in common is that each is formally innovative. Each begins by working within the conventions of a specific genre, only to depart quite radically from them. Even more important is the fact that the formal innovation points to a historical situation that can only be felt and understood in some new and original way. We can use these films to exemplify and extend the general observations that have been made about Hong Kong cinema—its adoption of spatial narratives to suggest dislocations, a new complexity in the treatment of affects and emotions, a creative use of popular genres, a new localism, and a politics that can only be indirect.

The genre that Wong uses in *As Tears Go By* is what is known in Hong Kong as the hero movie, after the Chinese title of the series of very popular films made by John Woo. (The English title of the series is *A Better Tomorrow.*) In the Hong Kong cinema, Woo can be considered to be the polar opposite of Allen Fong, and not only in commercial terms. We must not hold John Woo's success in Hollywood against him, as his contribution to Hong Kong filmmaking is considerable. While Fong goes for a relatively pure "realist" image, Woo introduces a "mixed image." In Woo's films, two qualities stand out: a fascination with extreme violence, often filmed in slow motion for emphasis, on the one hand; and on the other, a plot that underlines the need for personal loyalties, usually between male friends, in a crumbling world. Action and affection are two distinct series, but they are two series that nevertheless interrupt each other, resulting in a mixed image. For example, in *A Better Tomorrow: Part I* (1986), Ho, one of the three main characters, intends to give up his lucrative career in crime for the sake of his younger policeman brother Kit. Ho is betrayed on his last job. Mark, Ho's friend and partner, avenges the betrayal in one of the classic shoot-out scenes of the Hong Kong cinema that so impressed Hollywood, and he gets crippled in the process. In both cases, it is the affection series that pushes the action series forward and eventually off course. Action therefore takes on a certain reflexivity and affection, an incipient note of violence. The limitation of the film, however, is that ultimately these two series interact without transforming each other. The moral and affective issues remain relatively simple. We do not find the moral ambiguities of film noir, much less those of disappearance. It has been said that Woo's hero films are allegories of the Hong Kong situation, the romanticization of the outlaw a displaced sign of resistance to Chinese rule. If so, they are allegories based on a *simplification* of the Hong Kong situation. Nevertheless, the twist in the genre that Woo introduced opened up new possibilities for other directors like Wong Kar-wai.

Up to a point, *As Tears Go By* follows quite closely the hero genre established by John Woo. One main part of the story deals with the friendship between two local hoods, the hero and his younger friend who still has to prove his mettle in the Hong Kong underworld. The friend is eventually manipulated by the gangs to carry out an assassination under conditions that could only prove fatal to him. The hero, unable to dissuade or protect him, simply follows him in a futile act of loyalty and gets shot, too. We seem to find here a link between action and affection similar to what we saw in the hero films. There are, however, a number of differences and complications, seen first of all in the way the film establishes an overall sense of spatial ambiguities and discontinuities that frames and undercuts the conventionalities of the story.

Consider, for example, the first shot of the film. As the credits are being shown, we see on the left-hand side of the screen a mainland Chinese department store with its neon-lit advertisement sign, while on the right, floating in the foreground, are multiple television screens, empty and flickering. In this single shot, two historically distinct spaces occupy one common ground: the physical space of the older kind of commodity—material, located in place, attached to a sign; and the televisual space of information, the new commodity—dematerialized, mobile, and placeless. The film will go on to develop these spatial ambiguities, for example, in its peculiar use of color and slow motion. Color is always either too strong or too weak, and the film looks by turns gaudy or pale, over- or underexposed, too red or too blue. The color is never just right. Similarly, action is so problematic that slowing it down reveals nothing further, certainly not a moral or cognitive point. The more slowly and carefully we look at something, the more puzzlingly it looks back at us, it seems. It is these *irresolutions*, both visual and cognitive, that marks Wong's film as a special kind of film noir: the *neonoir* of a colonial subject caught in the confusions of colonial space (a point I shall return to presently). Violence may always be threatening to erupt, but it is never straightforwardly celebrated as the voluntaristic act of an individual subject, as in John Woo's films; rather, it exists as a ubiquitous and unavoidable dimension of urban space itself, which offers the individual no choice.

When we turn now to the other main part of the story, the love relation that develops between the hero and the heroine, we see how affectivity, too, is shaped by these spatial constraints. The hero moves back and forth throughout the film between lover and friend: from Lantau Island, a quiet undeveloped part of Hong Kong where the heroine lives, to the mean streets of Mongkok where the hero's friend is always in trouble. Scenes of lovemaking are always interrupted by messages of violence in a disconcerting cadence, so much so that one can become fused and confused with the other. For example, Wong shoots the kiss in a phone booth between Maggie Cheung and Andy Lau—one of the most erotic scenes in Hong Kong cinema—in the same way that he shoots the fight scenes: both these scenes erupt suddenly, it is a violence that comes apparently out of nowhere, and both are shot in slow motion. Slow motion, however, is not being used (as it is by John Woo) to romanticize or aestheticize either love or violence; it is used analytically to study, to understand. But analysis by slow motion, like analysis by blowup, leads at a certain point only to a blurring of the image, that is, to bewilderment rather than to understanding. The closer you look, the less there is to see. It is as if for Wong the gangster film, with all its clichés, somehow became an exercise in a hopeless epistemology, the demonstration of a visual aporia, as if every shot had to be closely attended to because things are always surreptitiously passing you by. This is the *déjà disparu*, a reality that is always outpacing our awareness of it, a reality that the film breathlessly tries to catch up with.

What is so remarkable about *As Tears Go By* is the way it manages to construct its images by drawing on and destabilizing the clichés and standard situations of the gangster film. What we notice most about the film—from the opening to the closing sequence where the death of the hero is intercut with one quick shot of a flickering memory of lovemaking—is its visual density. But, as I am suggesting, it is not a visual density that coheres or allows us to map out an intelligible space. Rather, the images disorient by refusing to stabilize. For example, the film ends, as so many in the genre do, with the hero's violent death; but in the final shot, although the hero is dead, the image of him continues to throb on, like a heartbeat, as if the image had acquired a life of its own.

There is one final point to be made, concerning the film's relationship to colonialism—a surprising point, perhaps, because no direct references to the problematic of colonialism or its critique are ever made. The critique is made obliquely in the film's treatment of visuality and in its relation to genre. In visual terms, colonial space might be thought of as working to promote a way of seeing that gives the visible and established the authority of the real. It constructs *a gaze* in which the real appears, and disappears, for a colonial subject. (We will return to this point when we discuss Hong Kong architecture.) Because Wong's film consistently gives us a form of visuality that problematizes the visible, it can be said to represent and critique such a space. It does this in its use of color and slow motion, but also in the way it produces a general sense of visual overload, seen, for example, in the running together of the fast and the slow; in the absence of transition between the idyllic and the brutal; in the choice of unusual camera angles that disorient, like shots directly from above or below. It is understandable why *As Tears Go By* has often been compared to MTV. But whereas visual overload in MTV usually functions to hold an audience's attention, in Wong's film it functions to suggest that attention itself cannot hold the *déjà disparu*. An oblique address to colonial space can also be read in Wong's particular relation to genre. If the formulaic demands of the genre of the gangster film imply colonization and self-colonization by clichés, and if subverting the formulaic is not viable for a number of reasons (such as the need to get financial support to make films), there is still a third possibility: that of doing something else within the genre, of nudging it a little from its stable position and so provoking thought. This is postcoloniality not in the form of an argument; it takes the form of a new practice of the image.

A film of a very different kind that does have an argument is Ann Hui's *Song of the Exile*, which is set in the domestic space of middle-class Hong Kong and focuses on the relation between a mother and daughter. One of the many interesting features of Ann Hui's film is that it takes us away from the largely male concerns of Hong Kong cinema (Wong Kar-wei is not exempt from this charge in his earlier films). *Song of the Exile* begins with the daughter Hueyin receiving an M.A. in media studies in London but failing to get an interview with the BBC (while her British classmate does). She decides to return to Hong Kong to attend her sister's wedding, and there she encounters her mother with whom she has never gotten along. There is a flashback to early days in Macau (lovingly re-created): memories of living with her grandparents, who dream of returning one day to China, of an absent father working in Hong Kong, of a very different mother—quiet, self-effacing, a dutiful daughter-in-law. What has she become now? Just as we thought this was going to be another film—yawn, yawn—about the clash between tradition and modernity, Chinese customs and Western ways, both Hueyin and the audience have a revelation: it turns out that the mother is in fact Japanese, that she met her husband during Japan's last days in Manchuria. All Hueyin's memories of the past and of her mother's behavior are reassessed in light of this knowledge. We have another flashback to Macau, to a past that looks the same but that is now understood differently. Hueyin realizes for the first time how difficult it must have been for her mother living as an isolated, oppressed subject in Chinese society, set apart by her customs (the grandparents always complained that her food was not hot enough) and by her ignorance of the language, which Hueyin misread as quietness. Within the domestic drama, then, we find a historical allegory of a colonial situation with a Japanese (traditionally, the Hong Kong image of the oppressor) as the oppressed.

The daughter's sentimental and political education continues in the second part of the film when she accompanies her mother to her hometown in Japan. And there it is the daughter's turn to go through the experience of being an alien in a strange country. In one scene she loses her way and wanders into a farm where she picks a tomato to eat. A farmer appears and shouts excitedly at her in Japanese. We know from the subtitles that he is warning her not to eat the vegetable because it has been sprayed with pesticides. She thinks that he is threatening to prosecute her for stealing and runs away. The more the farmer runs after her to warn her, the harder she tries to run. Ignorance of the language makes her believe that she is a criminal. The episode ends happily, though, as they eventually meet the village's English-speaking schoolteacher who explains everything, just as the film itself ends happily with mother and daughter returning together to Hong Kong, having finally achieved some kind of understanding of each other. The mother now regards Hong Kong as her only real home, while Hueyin finds work as a producer at a local television station. In a coda, Hueyin goes to Guangzhou to visit her grandparents who had indeed returned to China, only to become victims of the Cultural Revolution.

In *Song of the Exile*, genre is transcended through the treatment of space and affectivity. We see this first in the presence of a structure that can be identified as the family romance, the fantasy that our parents must be more interesting or worthy than our actual parents. This fantasy about origins is most evident in Hueyin's attitude to her mother in the early part of the film, but it can also be seen in some form in her grandparents' idealization of China and her mother's identification with her native Japan. In the film the personal is political, and understanding one's mother and one's own personal history is the precondition for understanding history and society, specifically Hong Kong history and society. Ann Hui has attempted to link the personal and the political before, for example, in *Starry Is the Night* (1988) about a woman's unhappy love affair with her married university professor and, many years later unbeknownst to her, with the professor's son. In this earlier film, the personal is identified quite weakly with erotic relations with the result that the political point is largely lost in sentimental confusions. *Song of the Exile* has a firmer structure, where the family romance is used as social allegory and functions to show the emotional confusions about "home" that result from a rapidly changing cultural space. These confusions of the family romance are finally overcome by Hueyin who can be reconciled with her mother, and by the mother herself who can be reconciled with the "loss" of her Japanese past, and both finally return to Hong Kong as home. The grandparents, on the other hand, who pursue the romance back to China, fail to overcome the past and suffer the consequences of their fantasy.

The film's narrative unfolds in a series of flashbacks, cutting back and forth between past and present. The originality of Ann Hui's use of the technique is that it does not just present to us a past that can elucidate the present through a chronological reshuffling. Rather, we are given a structure that is more spatial than chronological: the flashback technique shows us a past and a present that do not quite mesh, that seem initially to contradict each other; but it is these discrepancies that force a reevaluation of both memory and experience. It is notable that as the film progresses, we begin to see not only flashbacks, but *flashbacks of flashbacks*, as memories themselves are reassessed and finally understood. So while the earlier flashbacks have a nostalgic tone of intense poignancy and puzzlement, it is replaced in the later flashbacks of flashbacks by a general tone of sympathy and understanding, as nostalgia itself is *mise-en-abîme*. In terms both of narrative and technique, the structure then is one of reconciliation, of puzzling experience illuminated by understanding.

The need for understanding is Ann Hui's principal theme. Here is the voice of liberal Hong Kong, which believes that the past and history itself can be changed through the overcoming of misunderstandings and prejudices. Her song of the exile is not a siren's song that leads to rash actions (as Wong Kar-wai's film largely is), but a rational song of reconciliation, a song about the end of exile through understanding. The position it castigates is that of people who hold on stubbornly to a situation that is no longer there, the most striking example being the mother's younger brother, the former war pilot who refuses to accept the fact that the war is over, preferring a life of bitter memories. Yet it is exactly here in the argument for the need for understanding that we find both the film's strength and weakness. It offers hope for understanding, but it does not address with sufficient clarity or take far enough the question of how the cultural space of Hong Kong can be understood or addressed. For example, on one level the film clearly situates Hong Kong in relation to other social-affective spaces—London, Macau, Japan, Manchuria, China—and suggests that Hong Kong as a place can only be constructed out of its shifting relationships with these *elsewheres*. Yet on another level, especially toward the end of the film, a simpler account of Hong Kong as a "home" that one can come back to, as a definite *somewhere* with its own internalized history, becomes dominant. Understanding, then, becomes based to a certain extent on simplification, both spatial and affective. As a result, despite all its insights (for example, that the grandparents' patriotism is a form of ethnocentricity) and its concern with social and political issues, *Song of the Exile* remains largely just another private story. And the reason for this, it seems to me, is that colonialism is not just a misunderstanding, and explanations alone (as in the pesticide-sprayed tomato scene) cannot make it go away.

There is still the coda to consider, where Hueyin after her Japan experience goes to Guangzhou to visit her dying grandfather. In this short final section, the film's strengths reassert themselves to some extent. This is because it puts aside the need to give an argument about reconciliation to leave us with a number of intensely felt but contradictory images. The first is that of the grandfather lying on his deathbed, put there prematurely by the Red Guards. But at this point, even after firsthand knowledge of some of the harsher realities of Chinese life, he can still say to Hueyin, "Don't lose hope in China." This scene is followed by one of the most striking images in the whole film. The grandmother has adopted a mentally disabled child to look after, and it reminds us of the early scenes in Macau when she lavished care on Hueyin. But as she is spoon-feeding him, he suddenly turns on her and literally bites the hand that feeds him. The image is striking because it seems to be not merely an image of ingratitude, but a glimpse of the darker, more inexplicable side of human life that mocks our claims to understand it. Finally, the film ends with two shots almost superimposed on each other: the first, a final flashback to happy days in Macau in the lotus ponds with the doting grandparents; the second, a shot of present-day Guangzhou, busy, energetic, with no time for memories. It is the inclusion of punctums like these, rather than the film's implied argument, that provoke thought and feeling.

Let me turn now to a third film, one of the great successes of the Hong Kong cinema: Stanley Kwan's *Rouge* (1988), which I will be comparing with his 1991 production *Center Stage. Rouge* is quite distinct from the two films just discussed, although it has some elements in common with them.

As with Ann Hui's *Song of the Exile*, in *Rouge* the history of Hong Kong as a city is woven into the stories of personal relationships. The film cuts back and forth between Hong Kong in the early 1930s and the late 1980s. As with Wong Kar-wei's *As Tears Go By, Rouge* uses genre, in fact, a mixture of popular genres. It has elements of the nostalgia film: the vanished world of the thirties—with its beautiful courtesans, dashing heroes, and baroquely elegant settings—is lovingly re-created. It can be taken as a sentimental story about star-crossed lovers. Fleur, the toast of Shek Tong Tsui (today, a rather shabby quarter of the Western District, but in the thirties the scene of Hong Kong's stylish and expensive local nightlife), falls in love with Chan Chen-bong (also known as Twelve Master), scion of a rich and respectable Chinese business family. The only resolution in the thirties to such a social mismatch is death, and they eventually agree to commit suicide together. This introduces the most clearly generic element into the film, the ghost story. Unable to meet up with Chen-bong in the afterlife, Fleur returns to the world after waiting for more than fifty years to look for him. She places an ad in a newspaper: "3811. Rendezvous at the usual place" ("3811" stands for March 8, 11 P.M., the time of their suicide). But Chen-bong does not show up at the appointed hour. The journalist Yuen who works at the newspaper and his girlfriend Ah Chor, a fellow journalist, decide after some vacillation to help Fleur in her search for Chen-bong.

Kwan's use of the ghost story genre can only be called inspirational. Hong Kong cinema has had a long history of ghost story films ever since the Kuomintang government banned the making of such films together with martial arts epics in 1935 in a campaign against superstition and moral decadence. The genre was given its contemporary form with Ann Hui's *The Spooky Bunch* (1980), which mixed comedy with horror, and Ching Siu-ting's *A Chinese Ghost Story* (1987), which introduced slick special effects. Kwan resorts neither to comedy nor to the use of special effects. Furthermore, even though the screenplay is based on a popular novel by local novelist Lee Bik Wah (who also scripted *Farewell My Concubine*), the film differs from the novel in important respects. Lee Bik Wah's *Rouge* is based on historical and literary sources and appeals to a traditional sense of the supernatural. The film downplays the supernatural in order to emphasize, through linking the figure of the ghost with woman and cinema itself, the even more contradictory dimensions of cultural space in contemporary Hong Kong.

For one thing, as a ghost, Fleur is presented with remarkable restraint (with none of the use of special effects found in popular ghost films). She can do none of the things that ghosts are supposed to do. She is distinguished only by her silk dress (the *cheong-sam*, rarely seen nowadays as daily wear), by certain mannerisms and old forms of expression, and by her formal style of makeup (emphasized in the film's opening shots)—a revenant who has just stepped out of a freeze-frame, "unchanged for fifty years," as Ah Chor skeptically puts it (an obvious ironic reference to the Sino-British Joint Declaration and the future of Hong Kong.) The supernatural is suspended in favor of the uncanny, which has quite different spatial implications. Instead of the supernatural, which registers the clear separation and incongruity of this world with the space of an otherworld, we find the mixed, heterogeneous space of the uncanny, where the unfamiliar arises out of the familiar and is a dimension of it: not another space but a space of otherness. The figure of the ghost evokes what David Harvey has called a "space-time compression."[12] Fifty years disappear into simultaneity while space in turn becomes heterogeneous and mixed. The result is that two periods of Hong Kong history are brought together in a historical montage. The paradox is that one of the most popular and fantastic of genres is used as a rigorous method of representing the complexities of Hong Kong's cultural space.

One of the striking features of this space caught by the film is a specific and unusual relation between old and new. What we find is not just a mixture of old and new, a point often made about the film, if by "mixture" is implied that old and new are still distinguishable one from the other, that the present simply includes residues, or ghosts (cf. Henrik Ibsen), from the past. Rather, what we find is a situation where old and new could switch places, and differences begin to blur. Consider once again the ghost as figure. It comes straight out of traditional folklore and can be taken as an example of old-fashioned superstition. (That essentially is how the figure is used in the Lee Bik Wah novel.) But the ghost as figure can also be seen in relation to that most contemporary of phenomena—the *cinematization of space*, where direct observation gives way to the authority of the media image: nothing is more ghostly than the high-definition electronic image. In Paul Virilio's words,

> from now on, we are directly or indirectly witnessing a co-production of
> sensible reality. . . . The direct observation of visible phenomena gives way
> to a tele-observation in which the observer has no immediate contact with
> the observed reality . . . the absence of any immediate perception of con-

crete reality produces a terrible imbalance between the sensible and the intelligible, one which can only result in errors of interpretation.[13]

Fleur is of course neither electronic image nor cyborg, but she shares one characteristic with them: under most circumstances, she is hardly distinguishable from real or living human beings. She may be a creature of the night, but then so are the habitués of the demimonde, just as Arnold Schwarzenegger's Terminator dressed in black leather is indistinguishable from the toughs of Los Angeles. The reversability of ghost and cinematic image parallels the reversability of past and present, knocking history into a strange loop.

What then at first looks like a series of flashbacks that contrasts past and present turns out in fact to be something more original. As in *Song of the Exile*, flashbacks do not just shuffle what in the end can be reconstructed as a linear narrative. In *Rouge* the effect of the cutting back and forth is to establish a *double temporal framework* for all actions, allowing "before" and "after" to chase each other. We see some obvious changes and discontinuities: a well-known theater has been replaced by a 7-Eleven, Ti Hung Lau (the pleasure house where Fleur worked) by a kindergarten. But the film also shows us a subtler kind of discontinuity—the discontinuity that appears as continuity. For example, trams and Chinese Opera have both continued to exist from the thirties into the eighties, but their functions, as means of transport or as popular entertainment, have changed. This kind of change within continuity is the most provocative aspect of the film—its uncanny or ghostly aspect. Moreover, it is in such a space that the film places the question of desire. The ghost story becomes a study of affectivity and the way it unfolds in a space of disappearance.

The film is shot in two contrasting cinematic styles. The Hong Kong of the thirties is represented by a camera style that lingers lovingly on every detail to give us a baroque world of wealth, leisure, and decadence, a theatrical world. Chen-bong first meets Fleur at Ti Hung Lau where she is singing a famous passage from a Cantonese opera, and their love develops in a similarly theatrical way. By contrast, the eighties are filmed in a neutral, unmarked, realist, demotic style to give us a mundane world of work, where the journalists Yuen and Ah Chor are too busy at work to have time to think about emotions. Chen-bong presents Fleur with a beautiful locket as a sign of affection; Yuen presents Ah Chor with a practical pair of athletic shoes. Yet once again what is crucial is not the contrast between an old-fashioned decadent world of pleasure and the contemporary realistic world of work and time. There is also a point of crossover, a chiasmus, between the two, situated, for example, in the notion of decadence—which could take different forms. Stanley Kwan has always been interested in the notion of decadence, and he has dealt with the notion in simplified form in his earlier film *Love unto Waste;* but in that film, decadence was no more than a general mood and moral tone. In *Rouge,* however, decadence reveals a complexity that challenges any easy moralizing.

For example, some signs of old-fashioned decadence might be the devotion to pleasure (including the pleasures of Cantonese opera), to opium, or to fine clothes. The world of Cantonese opera (which permeates the film on the soundtrack) may be associated with tradition: we see that Chen-bong's tradition-bound father who vetoed his marriage to Fleur is an aficionado. But opera is also associated with a world of absolutes, where kings can value a beloved wife over a kingdom. Fleur's theatricality combines the obsolete and the absolute in a way that is unfortunately not true of Chen-bong. He serves an apprenticeship in Cantonese opera but, significantly, does not finish it, in the same way that he can smoke opium for pleasure but not die of it. By contrast, for Fleur even clothing itself is coded in the language of tradition and the absolute. There is a scene where Fleur has tea and a tête-à-tête with Chen-bong's mother, hoping to be accepted as a future daughter-in-law. The mother treats her with great courtesy and makes her a "reasonable" proposition: she would be quite acceptable, even welcome, as a mistress, but not as a wife. She is then asked to model a wedding dress for the intended wife the parents have chosen—in other words, she can "model" for a wife but cannot be a real wife. It is Fleur's refusal to compromise, to be a surrogate wife, that leads to the suicide. In this decadent world, love can be either a game, negotiable in monetary terms (as in that wonderful scene played with Tse Yin, a veteran of the old Cantonese cinema, where every touch and caress has a price tag), or it can be deadly serious.

On the other hand, the fast-paced world of today is slow in its affective responses. The purposefulness and busyness go together with another kind of decadence: a form of emotional inertia. That is why the love between Fleur and Chen-bong both attracts and appalls the contemporary couple. Their sympathy for Fleur keeps fluctuating. Such passion demands an absolute commitment that they are either unwilling or unable to make. For example, there is one scene that shows Ah Chor and Yuen erotically aroused by their *discussion* of Fleur's affair, and they end up making passionate love. But after the lovemaking she asks him in a voice-over: Will you commit suicide for me? No, he says. And you for me? he asks. No, she replies. The uncompromising nature of passion appears to them to have a sinister side to it. This emerges as we learn the details leading up to the double suicide. Not only did the lovers swallow raw opium together, but Fleur also put sleeping pills in Chen-bong's wine without his knowledge. This makes Ah Chor accuse Fleur of being a murderess, and she drives Fleur from the house. However, on reflection Ah Chor relents, as she realizes that her anger stems from her jealousy of a passion that she lacks: "It is difficult to be a woman. . . . Who among us has her passion?" In contrast to the old lovers, the contemporary lovers, like contemporary Hong Kong society, find it difficult to commit themselves as they flounder in a confusion of values. Fleur's ghostly passion challenges the noncommittal emotional attitudes of Yuen and Ah Chor. They become more and more deeply involved in Fleur's search for Chen-bong because they glimpse that the outcome will affect their own relation to desire. "We are as anxious to see Twelve Master as you are," Ah Chor tells Fleur toward the end.

The film, however, does not correlate the space of the old and the new with the moral forms of commitment and compromise. These four terms circulate and produce a number of different permutations. Nor is it a question of a choice of space. This comes out in the ironic ending, where we meet Chen-bong again, the only character who is situated in both spaces. We learn that not only did he survive the suicide attempt; he went on to marry a respectable woman whom he did not love, to squander the family fortune, and to survive into the present as a physical and spiritual wreck, working as a film extra. The implication, therefore, is that even in the most intense love there is misjudgment, error, weakness. The cultivation of personal intensities as a refuge from a morally imperfect world that demands constant compromise cannot avoid contamination from such a world. "Who wants to die?" Ah Chor asks Fleur, speaking for survival and in defense of Chen-bong—and of herself. But then Chen-bong's survival is also his form of punishment for not keeping faith. One might read the ending as posing a problem about action and conduct in a Hong Kong uncertain about how to deal with its future, a problem that has as yet no resolution.

The other outstanding film by Stanley Kwan is *Center Stage* (1991; a.k.a. *Actress* in the United States, and *Ruan Lingyu* in Chinese). It is a film biography of Ruan, the most charismatic star of the early Chinese cinema that was based in Shanghai, and it follows her life from 1929 when she was only nineteen (but already regarded in film circles as being "better than Wu Dip," another legendary actress) to her suicide in 1935, hounded by a former lover and the press. It is, however, film biography of a special kind, and although it seems at first sight a very different kind of film from *Rouge*, with its partial use of documentary methods rather than a ghost story, the two films have a lot in common, particularly as regards the innovative use of genre.

The official details of Ruan's life are well known, and the film recounts them quite faithfully. It is a story of Cinderella in the new age of media. Born in 1910 in Shanghai to parents from Guangdong, Ruan was six when her father died. Her mother went into domestic service with the rich Zhang family, which enabled Ruan to be educated at a famous Shanghai girls' school. At sixteen, she fell in love with the seventh son, Zhang Damin, but parental objections prevented them from being together until the parents died. Subsequently, Zhang lost the family fortune in poor business deals, and Ruan became an actress and supported the philandering Zhang. She also adopted a daughter. After acting in a number of mediocre films (the prints of which are now lost), she got her first important role in 1929, and a string of popular and critical successes followed. Her private life was less happy. She broke off with the feckless Zhang (who demanded "alimony" from her) and started living with the business tycoon Tang Jishan, who not only had a wife in the country but also a history of affairs with film actresses. The crisis came in 1935 after Ruan had finished the film *New Woman* with the progressive director Choy Chor Sang. The film was a biography of a woman writer who, abandoned by her husband and unable to make a living from her writing, turned to prostitution to support her child. The film also showed how the yellow tabloids drove her eventually to suicide by printing scandalous reports about her life. This infuriated the Shanghai press, which made sure the film was censored and took every opportunity to attack Ruan, the star. Zhang was paid to publish the story of his life with Ruan, and in his account he also charged her and Tang with adultery. Under constant pressure from Zhang and the press, Ruan finally committed suicide on 8 March 1935—which also happened to be International Women's Day, as well as the date of Fleur's suicide. She left behind an open "Letter to the Public," in response to which Lu Xun wrote an essay that used a quotation from Ruan's letter as his title: "Gossip Is a Fearful Thing." The story as it has come down to us is about the tragedy of a beautiful and talented woman destroyed by the power of the press and by a patriarchal society. In his film, Kwan includes a scene where Ruan turns in desperation to the progressive director Choy, who refuses to go away with her because he, too, has a mistress in Shanghai and a wife in the country.

These official details, however, are merely the starting point of the film by Kwan, whose main interest we soon see is not biography but something quite different: the investigation of a legend. The film begins with a number of haunting stills from Ruan's early films, all copies of which have disappeared. This sets the tone and serves to underline from the outset a point made once again by Paul Virilio when, writing about the "mysterious star system, which becomes essential to the young spectacle industry," he observed that "the star is only a spectre of absorption proposed to the gaze of the spectator, *a ghost that you can interview*."[14] Ruan, the greatest star of all, is still remembered more than fifty years after her suicide: she is, as Maggie Cheung who plays her in the film says, a legend. But the condition of being a legend is a certain ghostliness, as fame is no more than the sum of misunderstandings gathered around a great name (as Rainer Maria Rilke said). The ghost as figure that we first saw in *Rouge* is recapitulated in another modality in *Center Stage* and used to study Ruan Lingyu as legend. (Interestingly enough, both "ghosts" return after fifty years.)

How then do we go about interviewing a ghost? Drawing on autobiography and personal experience, as Ann Hui did in *Song of the Exile*, is obviously inappropriate. Rather, Kwan introduces a double structure by adopting a quasi-documentary style on top of the fictional film narrative, a structure that parallels the double temporal framework in *Rouge*. Also as in *Rouge* something unusual happens with this structure: the functions assigned to documentary and to fiction film are the reverse of their more usual functions. It is the fictional or narrative part of the work that recounts the known facts of Ruan's life, while it is the documentary part that provides the elements of speculation and exploration. If the "official story" documents only the stuff of legend into which Ruan herself disappears yet again, then something else must be introduced to disturb this fatal structure. Hence all those interviews with the present-day actresses Maggie Cheung and Carina Lau (who plays Li Lili, Ruan's contemporary) where they compare their own experiences of stardom with those of their predecessors, or all the interviews with Ruan's surviving contemporaries or with her biographers and hagiographers. The point of this kind of documentation is not to establish the facts, which are only too much there, but to interpret them, to speculate about them. The documentary style is not used for greater realism (unlike in the work of Allen Fong); rather, it introduces a certain heteroglossia and allows other voices to be heard: snatches of Cantonese and Mandarin, as well as Stanley Kwan's own voice as interviewer/interrogator.

A large part of *Center Stage* is devoted to showing Maggie Cheung recreating famous scenes from Ruan's films made between 1929 and 1935, where a lot of attention is directed to the craft of acting. For example, we see Cheung as Ruan asking a friend about the painful experience of childbirth and then lying down in the snow to prepare for a scene in a 1929 film about a destitute mother protecting her child in the snow. Or we see Cheung as Ruan in the final deathbed scene of *New Woman*, struggling to get the expression right, being told by the director to draw on her own experiences. These scenes by Cheung filmed in color are then juxtaposed with the performances by Ruan preserved in black and white prints. The point about this procedure does not seem to be to establish the remake as a more or less successful pastiche of the original, or to emphasize the unassailable authority of the archive. Nor are the reconstructions of Cheung as Ruan preparing for a scene, by connecting the required emotion to her "real-life experience," a recommendation of the artistic merits of method acting. Rather, this attention placed on acting and filmmaking makes the following point: in a very real sense *Ruan Lingyu is her acting*. It is not a question, therefore, of looking for a person behind the acting or conversely of identifying the person with the dramatic role: these are merely the most pathetic of fallacies, responsible for creating legend and gossip, turning an actress into a ghost. Rather, it is a way of representing the ghost as an actress.

What *Center Stage* poses, therefore, are the related questions of how to look at Ruan's films today and how to look at film culture in general. But these questions of form arise out of a cultural space where the act of looking itself is both the most developed and the most problematic act of all. Stanley Kwan's obsession with ghostly figures in his two best films turns out to be a method of evoking and representing critically the space of the *déjà disparu*.

3

Wong Kar-wai: Hong Kong Filmmaker

The argument in the previous chapter is that Hong Kong cinema both produces and is produced by a specific cultural space, and therefore our response to and evaluation of individual films have to take this into account. Moreover, it is a space of the *déjà disparu*, of disappearance, one characteristic of which, particularly significant for cinema as well as for architecture, is the problematic nature of visuality. "That which is merely seen (and merely visible) is hard to see," Henri Lefebvre notes about what he calls the "abstract space" of neocapitalism.[1] The point holds true for the space of the *déjà disparu*, where the visual is both ineluctable and elusive at the same time. Disappearance is certainly the result of speed, understood both as the speed of historical changes and as the technological speed of information and communication. But it is also the (negative) experience of an invisible order of things, always teetering just on the brink of consciousness. And it is this "lived" experience of the negative, something we are never, ever sure we are experiencing, that can be called the contemporary form of the colonial and that the new Hong Kong cinema describes. Hong Kong cinema can intervene in political debates more effectively by problematizing the visual than by advancing direct arguments about identity.

One reason for this is that the *déjà disparu* presents special problems for representation. It defeats good intentions by making them look tendentious. For example, this is what makes a film like Evans Chan's To Liv(e) with its pretentions to topicality relatively unconvincing. The film uses Hong Kong's controversial policy of forced repatriation of Vietnamese boat people as an occasion for pleading a case for Hong Kong's special position. This is correlated with a depiction of the personal problems of a Hong Kong family with "traditional" parents and "progressive" Westernized children: the daughter has a relationship with an "artist," the son with an older, divorced woman of whom the parents disapprove. The result of all this "realism" is something curiously static and abstract, one symptom of which are the shots of the Hong Kong skyline that focus on all the recognizable architectural landmarks, that is, on the visible and established. The liberal sentiments expressed in the film cannot prevent it from sounding like an apologia for Hong Kong identity. But any apologia that does not confront the aporias of Hong Kong's cultural space, or that gives only a positivist account of Hong Kong identity, does not go far enough. From this point of view, we see that Stanley Kwan's obsessions with urban ghosts and legends and Wong Kar-wai's systematic irresolutions are so many strategies of representing the déjà disparu indirectly and negatively through the mediation of genre and the provocation of fantasy. It could also be said that their works, which have no overt political content, are, from the perspective I am sketching out, the most political of all, insofar as they describe mutations, particularly of space and affectivity. Defending the cinema of Roberto Rossellini, Yasujiro Ozu, and Jean-Luc Godard against Marxist critics who have attacked their films and their characters "for being too passive and negative, in turn bourgeois, neurotic, marginal," that is, apolitical, Gilles Deleuze writes: "Godard says that to describe is to observe mutations. Mutation of Europe after the war, mutation of an Americanized Japan, mutation of France in '68: it is not the cinema that turns away from politics, it becomes completely political, but in another way."[2] Similar arguments can be made about the politics of Hong Kong cinema after 1982, which describes the mutation of disappearance.

Perhaps the first four films of Wong Kar-wai constitute, to date, the most wide-ranging exploration of Hong Kong's problematic space. We have already discussed As Tears Go By and Wong's use of the gangster genre, his critique of both visuality and the masculinist ethos, as well as his depiction of a generalized and abstract violence, beyond fistfights and gunfights, to which the characters finally fall victim. I want now to consider his next three films: Days of Being Wild (1990), Chungking Express (1994), and Ashes of Time (1994). It is an unpredictable series, with each new film a departure from the last, yet no one quite starting entirely ab initio, from scratch. The four films do form a series, though a heterogeneous one. Each starts with the conventions of a popular genre—and deliberately loses its way in the genre.

When *Days of Being Wild* was released in 1990, it was reputedly the most expensive film ever made in Hong Kong. With the commercial success of *As Tears Go By* behind it and a cast of Hong Kong's top stars, audiences expected something spectacular. Wong's second film is set in Hong Kong of the early sixties, which seemed another good move, given the current interest in Hong Kong history. The English title alludes to films about youthful rebellion like Stanley Kramer's *The Wild One* (1954) with Marlon Brando in a leather jacket on a motorcycle, or to David Lynch's more re- cent road film *Wild at Heart* (1990). The Cantonese title, *The Story of Ah Fei*, seems even more explicit. It was the Chinese title given to Nicholas Ray's classic *Rebel without a Cause* (1955). The term *Ah Fei* means a rebellious youth. The name derives from a standard recrimination that Chinese par- ents direct at the too-independent young: "[Now that you] have [grown] feathers and wings, [you] can fly [away]." *Fei* means to fly, and *Ah Fei* has a stronger nuance of ingratitude and delinquency than the term *rebel*. In Wong's film, Ah Fei as rebel and highflier has an obvious if ironic relation- ship to the myth that the main character Yuddy recounts about the legless bird who has to keep flying or die. In the myth, flying is necessary to sur- vival. However, the film's title raises certain generic expectations that the film disappoints, in much the same way that the story of the legless bird gets exposed toward the later part of the film as merely an example of Yuddy's own self-serving myth. Not only is there no glorification of rebel- lion and action; there is very little of either rebellion or action to be seen in the film at all. Yuddy understands at the end that the legless bird that holds to the romance of movement does so not because he has a boundless energy but because he is stillborn.

Genre is still important, but it is used in a risky way: to raise expecta- tions that are not fulfilled. The story of the legless bird has a structure that is paradigmatic of much in the film: it is the structure of the imploded myth, the structure of disappointment. Take, for example, the construc- tion of the lovers' time, the one minute before 3 P.M. on 16 April 1960 when Yuddy and Lai Jun first became "friends" and subsequently lovers. That public minute that recurs every day becomes a special moment in the lovers' private time, like a daily appointment with the origin of passion. But in the film, all appointments are dis-appointments. Passion dies and private time is swallowed up once again and becomes indistinguishable from public time, no matter how wilfully one or both lovers try not to forget. Disappointment means that the subject is no longer identified by memory or time, hence the constant references to private memory and public time, which nevertheless fail to define or individualize personal intensities, and hence the introduction of a serial structure of repetition (which we will be considering presently). Another example of disappointment: the policeman who consoles Lai Jun after her affair with Yuddy waits in vain for her to call him at the public phone booth that he passes on his beat every night around the same time; when she does call, he is no longer there, having left the police force and joined the merchant navy after his mother's death. In a third relationship, that between Yuddy and Mimi, we find Mimi very curious about Yuddy's foster mother's apartment where he grew up. He never allows her to visit, but when she does have a chance to see the inside of that apartment—after he has left her—she can only say that it is nothing special. One other example must be mentioned: the great panning shot of dense green forests that introduces the film. Just as we begin to think it is an image that signifies pure nature or unspoiled origins, we notice some lines that cross the screen that are gradually discernible as electric wires or telephone lines: nature has disappeared. Disappointment then is a consequence of the mistaking of signs.

There are two instances of conventional violence in the film: one when Yuddy beats up his foster mother's gigolo, and the other when a fight breaks out with a gang of toughs in the Philippines. But most of the film is taken up with permutating the sets of possible relations among the six main characters in a series of affective tableaux. This serial structure of repetition, exchange, and transference seems to have an independent life of its own. It binds the characters, smothers the violence, and limits the possibility of rebellion. If rebellion usually implies breaking off from the binds of a system and moving in a new direction, even if it involves a certain destructiveness, in Wong's film there is no way of breaking off from the series. All affective binds are double binds that inhibit movement, and so destructiveness gets largely internalized. In classic examples of rebellion like *Rebel without a Cause*, there are at least some moments of happiness, however short-lived; but in Wong's film there are no images even of pleasure, only instances of proximity without reciprocity. The characters miss each other and fail to "match up," as Yuddy's friend Wu Ying (the Fly) tells Mimi, after he has sold the car that Yuddy had given him because he looked out of place in it, just as he is no match for Mimi herself. As a result, no story has a happy conclusion, and everybody comes off second best. Love then is either entirely selfish and exploitative (Yuddy and his foster mother); or it is a boringly predictable sequence of friendship, sex, co-habitation, and marriage to be avoided at all costs (Yuddy and Lai Jun); or it is a struggle for domination, a competition about who cares less (Yuddy and Mimi); or it does not even arrive at the stage of being a relationship (Lai Jun and the policeman, Wu Ying and Mimi).

At the center of the series, it would seem, is Yuddy, who has an important and dominant relationship with each of the main characters. The first shot of Yuddy shows us his back. At critical moments, usually when a relationship is ending, he combs his hair. Yuddy is indifferent and narcissistic, a self-sufficient character in a world of the emotionally needy. "I don't know what he is thinking," Mimi tells Wu Ying, "but I know very well what you are thinking." It is his air of emotional independence that makes Yuddy look so seductive. Yet it becomes quite clear that for all his studied indifference Yuddy is the most needy and dependent of all, an abandoned child raised by a foster mother, obsessed with knowing the identity of his biological mother. He does no work and has been supported all his life by his foster mother. "What's the difference," she asks him after he has beaten up her gigolo, "between paying you and paying him? He gives me more pleasure." This pattern of dependency that shows itself as independence is repeated with Mimi. That is why he angrily throws her out of his apartment when she naively offers to support him by becoming a dance hall hostess, an offer that threatens to destroy his illusion of self-sufficiency. When his foster mother finally tells Yuddy the whereabouts of his biological mother, he drops everything, including his relationship with Mimi, to look for her in the Philippines. His mother refuses to receive him, and we have another shot of Yuddy, very similar to the early shots, as he walks away from her estate, determined not to turn his head. The obvious pairing of these shots shows that self-possession is just the other face of a sense of loss. At this point, we have another shot of the dense green forests that we saw at the beginning of the film. The forests can now be placed specifically in the Philippines and connote a mother and an origin that Yuddy cannot find, something that the presence of the telephone lines in the first shot ironically prefigure. The more developed the lines of communication, the more tenuous the lines of intimacy.

Dependency that looks like independence is one instance of the film's overall structure of disappointment. It makes Yuddy's search for his mother not just another straight allegory of an obsessive search for origin and identity. The structure of disappointment ironizes all notions of origin (mother) or identity (home) and empties allegories of meaning. Finding his mother in the Philippines also means losing her. We see therefore that the film does not so much avoid allegory as *voids* it. But it is also this voiding that saves it from some of the sentimentalities of Ann Hui's *Song of the Exile*. If history becomes meaningful for Hueyin in the Japan where her mother was raised, history becomes hysterical for Yuddy in the Philippines where his mother lives. He gets drunk in Manila's Chinatown, loses his papers and all his money to a prostitute, and tries to cheat some Filipino thugs out of a fake passport without paying for it, an act of self-destruction. They catch up with him on the train leaving Manila and shoot him. The dominant center of the affective series turns out to be an empty center.

The skewing of affectivity, seen most dramatically in Yuddy but also in all the other characters, should not be taken as a sign of individual pathology. It is also the negative and mystified response to an abstract space of disappearance. The skewing of affectivity is the only "content" and displaced index of such a space. It is a space that is at once very much there (in the effects it can produce) and not there (as directly discernible cause). For example, all intimate relationships are mediated by structures alien to the cultivation of intimacy—whether it is clock time, or objects like the pair of expensive earrings that Mimi covets at her first meeting with Yuddy, or the money that Yuddy's foster mother spends on her gigolo or that Yuddy's real mother pays to his foster mother for his upkeep. That is why, even at moments when one would expect intimacy, the characters are curiously out of touch with one another.

The space of the *déjà disparu* also has an effect on a larger experience of time and history. The film is set in the sixties, which on one level it painstakingly re-creates by paying close attention to period detail. It shows us the brand of cigarettes popular at the time (Craven A); the once popular Queen's Cafe, which served a Hong Kong version of Russian food; the clothes and watches people wore or the cars they drove. Even the film's color, with its sepia tones, looks a little like old photographs. But the film is not merely a pastiche of the sixties, defining history in terms of style and image. There is also the soundtrack, which adds an important dimension to the temporal structure. The soundtrack consists of ballroom favorites like "Always in My Heart," "Perfidia," and a well-known Chinese song. These songs in fact predate the sixties, and even when they were played then, they were already *out of date*. If the visual details locate a time, the soundtrack dissolves it back into prior moments. The result then is a history of the sixties that, like the experience of disappearance itself, is also there and not there at the same time. The film does not give us Hong Kong in the sixties viewed from the nineties, but another more labile structure: the nineties are to the sixties as the sixties are to an earlier moment, and so on and on. This may be why the film ends on a David Lynch-like note of suspension, by introducing an unknown character out of nowhere in the final few minutes. We see him in a room with an extremely low ceiling. He finishes dressing, combs his hair, puts money and a deck of cards in his waistcoat pockets, and then switches off the lights, while all the time the anachronistic music is heard in the background.

With a slight shift of perspective, it is possible to see the problematic as the comic, and to emphasize the humor inherent in a skewed space. This is exactly what Wong does in his third film, *Chungking Express*, which is his version of the romantic comedy genre. It is comedy that retains a tough urban edge, set in the jungle of the big city (the Chinese title literally translated is *Chungking Jungle*). The action revolves around the notorious Chungking Mansions, a kind of down-market-mall-cum-flophouse, with cut-price shops operated mainly by Indians, cheap curry joints, pimps, and whores. Located right in the middle of Tsimshatsui, Hong Kong's major tourist spot, it is a truly heterotopic space and living contradiction. In Chungking Mansions, Wong places the Midnight Express, a fast-food stall that the characters in the film patronize, whence the English title Chungking Express, a portmanteau term for a portmanteau space.

The film is split into two narrative and stylistic parts, with the fast-food stall as some sort of anchoring point. The first involves a cop, He Qi Wu, at the point of being jilted by his girlfriend, May, and recounts his encounter with an attractive blonde-wigged female gangster. The second part concerns another cop, #663, who is also in the process of being thrown over by a flight attendant, and follows his developing relationship with the impish Ah Faye who works in the fast-food stall. In these stories, the counterposing of space and affectivity, so painful a part of Wong's first two films, is still there, but given a comic, even affectionate turn. The tone is set by the first few shots of the film. They show a Hong Kong just before dawn together with He Qi Wu's voice-over: "We rub shoulders with each other every day. . . . We may not know each other. . . . But we may become good friends someday." Wong's shots of the city and even of Chungking Mansions itself give us visual fragments that require a certain effort to construe, not clichéd images of the Hong Kong skyline or unified wholes. It is true that people in Hong Kong, like the city itself, may be seen but not known; the situation is still one of proximity without reciprocity, except that this state of affairs does not completely exclude the growth of intimacy, even if it is an intimacy that takes idiosyncratic forms. The result is a special kind of comedy that has the distinction of being both very specific to the Hong Kong situation and at the same time never seen before in the Hong Kong cinema.

When we think about films that make comedy out of neurosis and urban malaise, the cinema of Woody Allen comes to mind. *Chungking Express*, however, is not *Manhattan*. Woody Allen focuses on a particular social type, the New York Jewish male with all his sociosexual hang-ups. In his films, Manhattan is not so much a place as a state of mind with ethnic and sexual overtones. The city is there very much as a backdrop to its strangely interesting people. By contrast, Wong's Hong Kong is not so much a mental or psychological state as it is a visual and spatial paradox, a skewed space that the characters have to adjust to emotionally, with comic results. Far from being the habitat of one social group, many different groups feel equally (not) at home in it; notice how in the first part of the film, Cantonese, Mandarin, English, Urdu, and Japanese are all spoken. It is as if it were the skewed space itself, and not just this or that visual, verbal, situational, or personal oddity that was producing the laughs.

Wong's comedy differs from the rest of Hong Kong's film comedy most of all in its visual style. All the best-known examples of Hong Kong comedy, like those made by the Hui brothers, rely heavily on stapstick and visual gags, following the premise recognized already by Georges Méliès in the early days of silent movies that the "cheapest tricks are the most effective."[3] This visual comedy has a kind of visceral immediacy. Wong's comedy operates on the different visual-comic principle that the seen is not the known. The images have a special quality: they all give the impression of being *throwaway* images. Thus in the first part of the film, images go by so quickly that we only catch glimpses of what is there, and in the second half what is there is not noticed by the characters or the audience because of a kind of reverse hallucination. For example, how many in the audience are at all aware that the three characters who get involved with one another in the second part of the film—the flight attendant, the policeman, and Ah Faye clutching a striped toy tiger—all made brief appearances à la Alfred Hitchcock in the first part? But they are there, presented in short oblique shots. Similarly, in the second part, we see Ah Faye rearranging the policeman's apartment when he is on his beat, but he does not notice anything out of place. What we find, therefore, is a principle of nonimmediacy and delay—which makes the title *Chungking Express*, with its connotation of the fast relay, now look more than a little ironic. The humor in the film is that of the double take, the delayed response. The joke is one that we laugh at only later.

One of the ways this comedy of delay works can be seen in the film's playing with styles, particularly Wong's own highly distinctive film styles used in his first two films. At many points, *Chungking Express* comes close to self-parody. For example, the use in the first part of exaggerated blues and reds, of slow-motion (step-printing) techniques, of quick cutting that makes action a blur—all this recalls the style of *As Tears Go By*, but now it is used self-consciously in a metastylistic way. All events therefore are mediated by a style that puts them at a distance and reduces their seriousness, including events like the assassination of the Indians and the American gangster. Similarly, part two begins with a scene that recalls the opening scene of *Days of Being Wild:* Policeman #633 smooths his hair with his hand (like the hero of *Days of Being Wild* combing his hair) and orders something over the counter from Ah Faye. But instead of a quiet and dreamy heroine, we see a hyperactive Ah Faye moving to the sound of "California Dreaming" playing at high volume, and instead of a self-possessed hero, just an ordinary guy ordering a chef's salad for his girlfriend who is about to abandon him or, as she puts it, cancel his boarding pass. The jokes at this level are of the nature of *in-jokes*, that is, jokes that are not perceived as such unless we are aware of the intertextual references.

There is also a constant doubling and pairing of names, objects, and people that elicits the response of the double take. For example, May 1 is the expiration date on a can of sardines that the American gangster gives to the blonde-wigged woman to remind her of her fatal deadline: the drug smuggling operation she is organizing has to be completed by that date. However, the operation goes wrong, and the Indian smugglers she hires and fits out with new clothes and shoes (made by quick-delivery specialists in Chungking Mansions) disappear at the airport. She tracks them down, shoots them, and then shoots the American gangster. But May 1 is also the expiration date on thirty cans of pineapples that the policeman Wu has been collecting one at a time since April Fool's Day, when his girlfriend May ditched him because he no longer reminded her of the Hollywood star of violent films, Bruce Willis. He sets for May his own private deadline of May 1 to come back to him. She does not, and he eats the thirty cans of pineapples in mourning for a faithless girlfriend, at the same time that the blonde-wigged woman is exacting retribution by shooting the faithless Indians. There are many coincidences of this kind as well as accidental collisions, like the one near the film's beginning showing Wu and the blonde-wigged woman bumping into each other before they become acquainted. "At our most intimate," Wu says, "we were only 0.01 cm apart"; they were closest at the moment when they did not know each other. There is the doubling of names: May is also the name of another young woman working at the fast-food stall whom the stall owner recommends to Wu. When he finally makes up his mind to date her, as a consolation for the lost May, she, too, has already gone away with another man. So on May 1 Wu lost two Mays in one night. The double take comes from the mistaking of signs, which is a constant pitfall when spaces seem to keep sliding into one another.

It is therefore not broad comedy that we find, but a comedy of details. The details multiply and replicate themselves; some are conspicuous, others blurred, but all have shifted slightly from their signifying frameworks. Thus freed, they are able to form new patterns and symmetries of their own. What makes the details comic is that they do not serve to define a mood or localize a situation; they are not the irreducible atoms of meaning, but merely the nodal points formed by converging and diverging lines of action and affectivity, small versions of heterotopic space, like Chungking Mansions itself. The details possess the paradoxical quality of *delayed immediacy*, Wong's version of *Nachträglichkeit*. The best illustration of this comedy of details comes in the second part of the film in Ah Faye's sly courtship of the policeman. After the flight attendant leaves him, we see him in a sentimental mood talking to the objects in his apartment: the thin cake of soap, the ragged face towel, the fluffy white doll, and so on. She also left his apartment keys in care of the fast-food stall. Ah Faye uses the keys to enter the apartment when #633 is out. She cleans and tidies it up; changes his soap, towel, toothbrush; buys goldfish for the fish tank; substitutes a yellow-and-black-striped toy tiger for his white doll, and Chinese black-bean mackerel for his cans of Del Monte sardines; leaves a photograph on his mirror; and so on. Still obsessed with the flight attendant, the policeman registers no surprise at the new objects, explaining them away as the result of a change in his emotional mood. He does not notice Ah Faye's presence in spite of all the clues she leaves him. "Lately, I've become more observant," he says to himself, as he eats from a can labeled Del Monte Sardines that now contains black-bean mackerel. It is only when he finally catches her in his apartment when he returns unexpectedly one day that he notices that she is there, much the same way that archaeologist Norbert Hanold finally sees that Gradiva materializes as Zoe Bertgang.

Related to the comedy of details is the comedy of the fetish, a displaced detail. A fetish is a substitute, a surrogate, a neurotic symptom, but it can also be regarded as a defense against neurosis, in that it is a less harmful kind of neurosis. All fetishes are potentially comic. Thus we see the characters in *Chungking Express* each with his or her own personal fetish.

For Wu, food (pineapples, for example) and jogging are defenses against emotional breakdown: jogging dissipates water from the body, leaving none for tears. With the blonde-wigged woman whose line of work is very risky, her fetish is the precaution of always wearing a raincoat and dark glasses at the same time: you never know when it will rain or shine, she explains. For Ah Faye, it is California, and for #633 it is women in airline uniforms. The only bad fetishes are those that other people impose on them, like the blonde wig that the American gangster wants all his women to wear. After he gets shot, the blonde-wigged woman throws the wig away; it is not her fetish.

The generally benign way of presenting the fetish also points to a major difference between *Chungking Express* and Wong's other films, namely, that it is in his comic film alone that we find images of pleasure and happiness. For example, Wu spends a disappointing night with the blonde-wigged woman (whom he finally meets at a bar) because she just sleeps through their time together in the hotel room. But when he leaves at dawn, he takes off and polishes her high-heeled shoes for her, and she calls him later on his beeper to wish him a happy birthday, which falls—when else?—on May 1. Similarly, Ah Faye does not keep her appointment with #633 at the California Restaurant in Lan Kwei Fong, deciding she has to go to the real California first, but she does send him an imaginary boarding pass she has drawn for him valid for the same time next year, which is like a kind of tacit promise to return. In these examples, there is a fleeting hint of a reciprocity that emerges from the delays.

We come now to Wong Kar-wai's *Ashes of Time*, made at about the same time as *Chungking Express*. This is a film based on the immensely popular martial arts stories of the Hong Kong writer Jin Yung, and it represents Wong's attempt at the kung fu film genre. As we would expect of him by now, he does interesting things with the genre by placing it in the cultural space explored in his previous films. For example, *Ashes of Time*, too, could be discussed in terms of its structuring of visuality, time, space, and affectivity. What is less expected is the uncompromisingly somber tone of the film, which the beautiful cinematography only tends to heighten. It is as if all the humor and lightness were concentrated on *Chungking Express*, leaving the traditionally extroverted, action-based martial arts film the task of telling a story about the weight of dead time.

The film does not obviously parody or ironize the conventions of the genre. Rather, the implications of the genre are followed through to their catastrophic conclusions, giving us in the end the complex continuum of a blind space and a dead time. The film's English and Chinese titles complement each other. While the English title puts the emphasis on time, the Chinese title puts the emphasis on space. It can be roughly rendered as "Sinister East, Malevolent West," which are the fearsome sobriquets of the two main heroes, but the title suggests as well the two points of a dystopic space. The film starts off by following the martial arts narrative convention of recounting stories of legendary heroes, highlighting their martial arts skills. Each of the four male heroes have a chance to display their fighting ability and courage. But there is a crucial change in the way heroism is represented. The more heroic the character the more he seems damaged by life; heroism is a form of sickness. The outstanding heroes (particularly the two heroes referred to in the film's Chinese title) are all in one way or another neurotics, living out their own private obsessions, which they project back onto the space around them. In this regard *Ashes of Time* has an affinity to psycho-Westerns like John Ford's *The Searchers* (1956) or Sergio Leone's *Once upon a Time in the West* (1969).

The ambiguities of heroic space can be suggested by considering how action is represented. The early fight sequence involving the film's main narrator Ouyang Feng, the Malevolent East of the title, typifies the pattern. It is no longer a choreography of action that we see, as in other kung fu or gangster movies, but a composition of light and color where all action has dissolved—a kind of abstract expressionism or action painting. What we find therefore is heroic space as both a space of power (as in architecture) but also as a kind of blind space that comes from an *excess* of light and movement, Maurice Blanchot's *la folie du jour.* Significantly, the third hero the film introduces is a swordsman on the point of going blind, whose last fight with a gang of horse thieves is a fight against the light. In all the fight scenes, it is only when the action slows down that light resolves itself into something recognizably human; but when we do catch a glimpse of a human figure, it is always at the fatal moment of dealing out death or in the throes of dying.

This blind space of heroism hides consequences from the characters. Heroism as a code of behavior is the ultimate phallic myth of power. It fosters the illusion that some consequential action is always imminent, which is what makes the characters forget that nothing happens, that life is over, that the time they live in is a dead time, a time of waiting rather than action. What the film shows, in defiance of the genre, is that between the brief moments of blind action are the long moments of waiting for something to happen. In *Ashes of Time*, time is a heavy weight/wait, a void to be filled if only by a dead body. There is a clear relation, then, between blind space and dead time: it is onto this dead time that the blind space of heroism has been displaced, and the stories of heroes now register these problematic new conditions.

Ouyang Feng best exemplifies what happens to heroic action in dead time. The film opens with him engaged in a heroic fight, but after this first fight that has taken place many years ago, the clean-shaven Ouyang Feng grows a beard (the ash of time, as it were), and we see him do no more fighting. Rather, he becomes a death broker, an entrepreneur who arranges killings and assassinations for a fee. He spends his time waiting on misfortunes, waiting for something to happen to other people, like a man whose life is over. However, while action is suspended, the memory of it is not so easily suppressed, and this takes us to the story of the seductive Huang Yaoshi, the Sinister East. He carries with him a bottle of choice wine (intended for Ouyang Feng) that is supposed to have the magical property of making those who drink it gradually forget the past. Unfortunately, heroism is a stimulant stronger than the numbing effect of any wine because it is none other than the phallic myth. The wine turns out to have no effect on memory. This amounts to saying that it is not possible to forget or leave behind the dead time as long as the phallic myth of action persists because one is doubled in the other.

This complex continuum of space (of action) and time (of waiting) means that it is not possible to simply associate the space of action with the male and the time of waiting with the female, as is usually the case in action films. In *Ashes of Time*, everybody waits. In spite of this, what persists is the *myth* of heroic male action that comes with the martial arts genre. What we see in the film is how men and women live their lives or construct their identities according to the expectations of the genre, however unreal these expectations have become in the much more complex space-time relations demonstrated everywhere else in the film. It is these false expectations, these ashes and residues, that destroy lives by skewing affective relations. And it is the pain of affect that is the index of something ungraspable, of a controlling space that is always already gone: the *déjà disparu*. Affectivity therefore is the other stage—bloodless but fatal—on which the "action" of the film unfolds.

The most dramatic example of this skewing of affectivity is the schizoid figure of Murong Yang/Murong Yin. She is first introduced dressed in man's clothes, a standard martial arts story convention. In this guise, she meets the seductive Huang Yaoshi, who flirtatiously says to her, after they have had a lot of wine together, that if she had a sister, he would certainly marry her. Murong Yang holds Huang to his promise and reappears as the lovely Murong Yin, but Huang does not show up at the appointed time. As Murong Yang again, she hires Ouyang Feng to arrange for Huang's assassination, but before Ouyang Feng agrees to accept the job, Murong Yin appears and offers to double his fee if he could have Murong Yang eliminated instead. Yang wants Huang killed to avenge her "sister's" disgrace; Yin wants Yang (her other self) killed to preserve the promise of happiness. Yin and Yang are deadlocked. Nothing can happen, and action moves elsewhere. In *Ashes of Time*, the affective reveals a problematic space controlled by a system of double binds where no real action can take place. In this respect it comes closest to *Days of Being Wild*, in spite of the many visual differences in the two films.

The pathetic figure of Murong Yang/Yin is just the most striking instance of an affective dysfunction that pervades the film as a whole, in less obvious and accordingly more dangerous forms. What fills the dead time are feelings of ressentiment—envy, jealousy, covetousness. Ressentiment can find expression in extremely contrasting ways: from the sexual asceticism of Ouyang Feng who lives like a hermit, to the Don Juanism of Huang Yaoshi, just as the physical space of the film is marked by extreme contrasts of desert and watery marshlands or lakes. Nothing, it seems, is more fearsome than feelings, and nothing is more destructive than a bad feeling. Ouyang Feng may have been a hero, but he could not speak words of love. This negligence wounds the woman he loves. She refuses to wait for him and exacts her revenge by marrying his brother. This act, as precise as a practiced sword thrust, turns her life into a bitter triumph and destroys his. Ouyang Feng changes from hero into cynical mercenary, the Malevolent East who profits from other people's misfortune. When a beautiful young woman asks him to help her avenge the murder of her brother by the gang of horse thieves and offers to pay him with a donkey and a basket of eggs, her only worldly possessions, he not only refuses but also suggests that she sell her virtue to raise more money. However, this is obviously not just greed, but an attempt to force on her an impossible choice: family honor or personal virtue? Ressentiment is also delight in seeing the humiliation of others.

Ironically, only the nonheroic figures are free of ressentiment. The example here would be the fourth swordsman introduced in the film, Hong Qi, the barefoot peasant. Ouyang Feng persuades him to put on shoes to raise his price as a mercenary, but this has no effect on him. He has made his way from his village with his sole possession, his camel, and his faithful and plain peasant wife has followed him against his wishes. Ouyang Feng does not succeed in influencing him. Eventually, Hong Qi helps the young woman with the eggs on a whim because he wants to, and he loses a finger in the process. This allows him to say to Ouyang: I am different from you; I can act because of a basket of eggs. When he departs from the desert to make his name in the field of arms, but unconventionally taking his peasant wife along with him, he is also departing from the heroic-romantic mode, if not quite breaking entirely with it. In a short afterword, we learn that Hong Qi later achieved fame as a swordsman and fought a duel with Ouyang Feng as a result of which they both died.

As in the other films of Wong Kar-wai, affectivity in *Ashes of Time* is the index of a space that cannot be grasped directly. It is a space I have called the *déjà disparu*, and it cuts across different genres and historical periods, being very much the negative ground against which both time and action are experienced. Hence the question of how these films relate to Hong Kong culture also cannot be directly posed. It is not as if there were already a Hong Kong culture in place that these films could be seen as representing in a relatively true or false way. Furthermore, they go beyond allegory to challenge the definition of Hong Kong culture itself by questioning and dismantling the way we look at things. And by describing mutations, they open up new possibilities.

4

Building on Disappearance:

Hong Kong Architecture and Colonial Space

Colonial Space and the Disappearance of History

The remark that Hong Kong reinvents itself every few years becomes quite credible when we look at the changing skyline of the Central District. This skyline may not yet rival that of New York or Chicago, but it is nonetheless highly impressive in its own way, with its growing number of signature buildings by international architects like Norman Foster, I. M. Pei, and Paul Rudolf. Such a skyline not only underlines the domination of the marketplace, with the architect's signature functioning as a brand name; it also takes to an extreme Sharon Zukin's argument that "market" erodes "place."[1] The combination of rising land prices, property speculation, and the presence of large corporations vying for prime space results in a constant rebuilding that makes the city subtly unrecognizable.

The most spectacular example of this might have been the Ritz-Carlton Hotel, located in the heart of Central. When it was nearing completion in early 1993, the original owners sold it to a multinational consortium, who reportedly played quite seriously with the idea of razing the luxury hotel to the ground before a single guest was registered, and putting in an office building instead because of the potentially higher income that might be generated. Buildings in Hong Kong suffer the fate of any other commodity, an insight that Walter Benjamin arrived at more than half a century ago: "In the convulsions of the commodity economy we begin to recognise the monuments of the bourgeoisie as ruins even before they have crumbled,"[2] an insight that is finally coming into its own. Property speculation means that every building in Hong Kong, however new or monumental, faces imminent ruin, on the premise of here today, gone tomorrow—a logistics that, by contracting time, dispenses even with the pathos of decay. The political slogans of the day—"Prosperity and stability" and "Fifty years without change"—are thus belied by an urban landscape that mutates right under our noses, making the question of spatial identity particularly problematic.

Architecture, because it is always assumed to be *somewhere*, is the first visual evidence of a city's putative identity. In this regard, the symbolic landscape of Central exerts a particular fascination, not only for filmmakers and photographers, but also for the domestic workers from the Philippines who take it over on Sundays when it is closed to traffic. But can the architecture of Central, or even the whole of Hong Kong architecture, represent the city? As Diana Agrest has pointed out, it is one thing to look at the city from the point of view of architecture and quite something else to look at architecture from the point of view of the city. The city from the point of view of architecture may be associated with painterly modes of looking derived from classical tradition, but architecture from the point of view of the city can only be associated with film, "the visual art that developed alongside the modern city,"[3] that is to say, the art that problematizes the visual as stable because it is film that gives us, in Jean-Luc Godard's words, truth twenty-four times a second.

In the case of Hong Kong, there is indeed an important relation between architecture and cinema that goes beyond including shots of impressive buildings on film. Not only are they the two most developed cultural forms in Hong Kong, but they are also the most dependent on the market and the most preeminently visual. Nevertheless, there is a crucial difference, and it concerns their relation to the visual. The Hong Kong cinema, in the work of its more interesting practitioners, uses the visual to problematize visuality itself and in this way contributes to a critical discourse on colonial space. The case of Hong Kong architecture, at least up to the present moment, is somewhat less sanguine. It constructs a visual space that to a large extent resists critical dismantling. In the cinema, the subject is surrounded by moving images, which requires even in its simpler forms a certain amount of critical attention to construe. By contrast, in the case of architecture, it is the subject itself that moves, around an image that is seen to be stationary (hence Agrest's point about the need to desta-bilize architecture through a cinematization of space). Architecture there-fore has the dangerous potential of turning all of us, locals and visitors alike, into *tourists* gazing at a stable and monumental image.

Insofar as it encourages a process of unreflective visual consumption, architecture in Hong Kong is the main material support of a space that can still be called colonial, in spite of official avoidance of the term *colony*. Colonial space can be thought of as the projection of a colonial imaginary that maps out a symbolic order in whose grids the real appears and disap-pears for a colonial subject. This amounts to saying that the formulation of a spatial problematic is becoming increasingly necessary to an analysis of colonialism exactly because colonial space in Hong Kong is quite specifi-cally a space of disappearance. In such an analysis, architecture has a cru-cial, if so far still negative, role to play. What this underlines, therefore, is the urgent need to develop a critical discourse on Hong Kong architecture and urban space, where the dominance of visuality is put into question, as in the case of the new Hong Kong cinema.

Let me elaborate on this notion of disappearance and the colonial gaze by referring to urban phenomena in Hong Kong that seem at first sight to stem from postcolonial sensibilities. The notion of disappearance I am al-luding to does not connote vanishing without a trace. In fact, it can go to-gether very well with a concern for presence and projects of preservation. In recent years, since the early 1980s in particular, there has been a grow-ing interest in what is self-consciously being called Hong Kong culture, which many read as Hong Kong's acquiring a sense of identity. For exam-ple, there has been a continuing vogue for photographic exhibitions about old Hong Kong; an archive of old Hong Kong films is just being estab-lished; studies of Hong Kong customs, traditions, and folklore are gaining all the time in academic respectability. It is in this context of preserving a cultural identity through preservation of cultural and urban forms that the strong response to the demolition of the Kowloon Walled City, that inner city of inner cities, must be understood. Because of a historical anomaly, the Walled City was a no-man's-land that fell outside British jurisdiction and beyond the administrative reach of China. The result was that it be-came a haven for all sorts of illegal and clandestine activities, although it was also just "home" to a number of ordinary people. When it was finally razed to the ground quite recently, an action made possible only through the approval of the Chinese authorities, there was a brief hue and cry, fol-lowed by the appearance of a glossy and expensive volume of essays and photographs commemorating it in all its seedy glory.[4] What can we make of this example? If colonialism goes together with a devaluation of local culture and identity, then it would seem that this new interest in the local is the symptom of an emerging postcolonial awareness. However, the situation is much more ambivalent than this, if we remember what Frantz Fanon pointed out a long time ago: "It is the colonialist who becomes defenders of the native style."[5] When the native style and culture are bracketed and separated out as a special category, they are effectively recontained and lose whatever potential they might have had to stir memory. Preservation, it should be noted, is not memory. Preservation is selective and tends to exclude the dirt and pain. Culture as preservation, which is what a lot that currently passes in Hong Kong for postcoloniality amounts to, can only be a form of kitsch, which Milan Kundera has graphically but accurately defined as "the absolute denial of shit, in both the literal and figurative sense."[6] Such denials make even the Walled City, with its traffic in drugs, prostitution, and human misery, look so glamorous—after the fact.

The preservation of old buildings gives us history *in site*, but it also means keeping history *in sight*. A critique of preservation is therefore also a critique of visual ideology. Let me take this argument about colonialism as a politics of the gaze a little further with the help of three examples of architectural preservation. It should be noted that the argument is not directed so much against preservation per se, which has its legitimate uses, as against the use of preservation as history to bring about the disappearance of history.

The first example is the Hong Kong Cultural Center, built on the site of the old Hong Kong-Canton railway terminal. The design of the cultural center offered an opportunity to imagine a community, but in the event, the opportunity was largely lost. The main structure that houses the auditoriums is one of those modernist placeless structures that could be from anywhere, looking like nothing so much as a giant ski slope. As if to compensate for the neglect of the local, one significant design detail was introduced. The clock tower in red brick from the demolished railway station was saved and incorporated into the overall design. On one level, this "quotation" from Hong Kong's architectural history is the expression of a sense of historical moment, giving to the cultural center a patina of local history. But on another level, this patina of history is no more than decorative, an *image* of history meant for visual consumption. In its relation to the overall design of the cultural center, the clock tower can be compared to that strange-looking, hard-to-construe, anamorphic object floating on the bottom of Hans Holbein's famous painting *The Ambassadors*, a painting that Jacques Lacan analyzed in his discussion of the gaze.[7] However, the difference between them is very significant and tells us something about how colonial space controls desire. Faced with *The Ambassadors*, the viewing subject caught in the gaze, that is, in the perspectival space that dominates most of the painting, cannot construe the anamorphic object as the representation of a skull. That is because the gaze is a channeling and socializing of desire, and it is such a desire that makes one space, the perspectival one, recognizable and turns the space of the anamorphic image into a hallucination. In the Hong Kong example, we have the opposite situation: the clock tower unlike the skull is seen *too easily* and is too quickly assimilated into the overall spatial ensemble (as an instance of "Hong Kong history"). Space is homogenized in the colonial gaze, as "old" and "new" are placed together in contiguity and continuity. There is also a spatial programming and socializing of desire, but it consists of making us accept, without shock or protest, the most blatant discontinuities as continuities. Any image preserved from the past may serve as a sign of a communal history. Such spatial practices are not very different from the practices of Disney theme parks, which also specializes in providing images of history. We are beginning to find equivalents of such theme parks in Hong Kong, like the Sung Village in Kowloon and the more recently opened Middle Kingdom—a re-creation in miniature of architectural monuments from China, which forms part of the Ocean Park complex. In these examples, as in the cultural center clock tower, an imaginary community takes the place of an imagined community. Culture as preservation leads not to the development of a critical sense of community but works to keep the colonial subject in place, occupied with gazing at images of identity.

The second example of preservation is Flagstaff House, an impressive colonial-style building constructed in the 1840s. First used as the headquarters of Jardine, Matheson, and Company and then as headquarters of the British military, it was later converted into a residence for the commander of the British forces. More recently, with the withdrawal of the British military presence in Hong Kong, there was some debate on what to do with the building. Eventually, the government's Architectural Services Department decided to preserve it by turning it into a museum to house a magnificent collection of Chinese teaware. This was done in 1984, and in 1989 the building was declared a monument. In this way, a historically significant building is saved from the bulldozers and the general public gets an education in Chinese culture. All sides, it would seem, stand to benefit from such an arrangement, and there is some truth in this.

However, there is a certain presumably unintended irony here, not only in the dates 1984 (the year of the Joint Declaration) and 1989 (the year of Tiananmen) but also in the historical associations that tea has with the Opium Wars and the British gunboat diplomacy that secured Hong Kong for Britain in the first place. This reincarnation of a British military establishment in the form of a museum of Chinese teaware skims over the monumental barbarisms of the nineteenth century by aestheticizing them out of existence. Flagstaff House could be read therefore as an example of the disappearance of history: not in the sense of history having come to an end, but in the sense of its *persistence along certain ideological guidelines*. Disappearance here implies the subsitition of one thing for another, a displacement of attention from the sometimes conflictual colonial history of Hong Kong, to the harmonious accommodation of Chinese culture in colonial architecture.

The third example is the Repulse Bay Hotel. This example may seem a little different from the first two, as it comes from the private sector, but the implications of preservation we find here are largely comparable. The original Repulse Bay Hotel, built in 1920, was a grand colonial-style building that became a famous Hong Kong landmark. With its wide verandah overlooking the bay, it was a fashionable meeting place for Sunday afternoon tea. In early 1982, at the height of land speculation, the hotel was torn down to make way for the building of luxury apartment blocks. The timing could not have been poorer because later in the year came Margaret Thatcher's visit to China. The immediate effect on the property market was a catastrophic slump in property prices, and the construction of the apartment blocks was delayed. Enter a movie director, Ann Hui, who wanted a few background shots for a film. A quick replica was built on the original site. This may have given someone the idea that a full-scale replica was a viable business proposition. As market confidence returned to Hong Kong in 1985 (as it has always done so far, no matter what the catastrophe), construction of the Repulse Bay apartment complex was taken up again, and a replica of the old hotel was included as an integral part. The project was completed in 1989, and it won Hong Kong's premium architectural award, the Hong Kong Institute of Architects' Silver Medal, partly for its successful integration between the "old" and the "new." However, the relation between old and new is very much like what we find in the cultural center, with much the same implications, except that in the case of the Repulse Bay apartment complex, the old is very clearly a remake, something that comes out of a movie set. The replica is not even, strictly speaking, an example of preservation, which is precisely what allows it to make more explicit what is only implicit in the two pre-vious examples: how preservation is posited on the disappearance of the historical site.

These instances of preservation are significant, even though preserva-tion is unlikely to be a major factor in Hong Kong's built space, because they exemplify the argument that the more abstract and ungraspable space becomes, the greater the importance of the image. Accordingly, in a space of disappearance, in the unprecedented historical situation that Hong Kong finds itself in of being caught between two colonialities (Britain's and China's), there is a desperate attempt to clutch at images of identity, how-ever alien or clichéd these images are. There is a need to define a sense of place through buildings and other means, at the moment when such a sense of place (fragile to begin with) is being threatened with erasure by a more and more insistently globalizing space.

The complication, of course, is that "place" and "space" cannot be op-posed in any simple way, nor can they be considered separately. It is clearly not possible to think of place merely in terms of definable physical characteristics and situatedness because the changing nature of space—that results from information technology, for example—inevitably entails a changing idea of place. Paul Virilio points out that the limits or bound-aries of the city itself have come into question, largely because of new informational and communicational technologies that introduce a novel idea of space: space, in an important sense, as nonphysical and demateri-alized. He makes the point by asking how one now gains access to the con-temporary city and answering: not through a city gate but rather through an electronic audience system: "The sound of gates gives way to the clat-ter of data banks. . . . the urban wall has long been breached by an infini-tude of openings and ruptured enclosures."[8] All major contemporary cities are thus "overexposed," as the idea of *boundary* is gradually replaced by the idea of *interface*. In the case of Hong Kong, it would seem that it has been primed for overexposure since its inception in 1841 as a British colony and a free port, where accessibility is an overriding consideration—a consider-ation that produces its own aporias. The large number of illegal immi-grants in the city shows how easily the border with China can be breached by land and sea. The difficulty of controlling smuggling (recently, of stolen luxury cars to the mainland) shows it is as easy physically to get out of the city as it is to get into it. Finally, the colony's by now definitive insertion into global networks of capital and information can therefore be seen as simply the latest episode in the relative devaluation of a physical idea of space *and* place.

On the other hand, even as place is being problematized by the new global space, it is nevertheless not the case that this space necessarily carries all before it. In this regard, Manuel Castells makes an essential point: "New information technologies do have a fundamental impact on societies, and therefore on cities and regions, but their effects vary according to their interaction with the economic, social, political and cultural processes that shape the production and use of the new technological medium."[9] In other words, there is a whole range of spatial and historical mediations to be accounted for, and this leaves room for a politics of built space, even if it is a question of building on disappearance. This amounts to saying that architecture cannot be separated from the spatial/ideological context in which it is produced. Let me begin then by presenting some of the idiosyncrasies of Hong Kong's urban space, which is that peculiar kind of colonial space that I call a space of disappearance, as a necessary preliminary to a discussion of its spatial politics.

Spatial Histories

The theoretical implications of disappearance have been explored most thoroughly in the writings of Paul Virilio, where disappearance is a consequence of processes of speed and digitalization that deprive forms and figures—whether paintings and sculptures or monoliths and architectural constructions—of their material support and physical dimensions: "Where once the aesthetics of the appearance of an analogical, stable image of static nature predominated, we now have the aesthetics of the disappearance of a numerical, unstable image of fleeting nature, whose persistence is exclusively retinal."[10] In relation to Hong Kong, however, a space of disappearance has specific local and historical references, which makes it possible to conceptualize it in several other ways as well.

In the first place, disappearance can be seen in relation to a recent cultural and political mood. There is something highly ambivalent about disappearance. It does not refer simply to the anxiety that the Hong Kong way of life will come to an end once Hong Kong is returned to China. It does not signify historical catastrophe *tout court* but is something more double-edged, the way an unprecedented and in many cases newfound interest in local culture and politics *appears* at the moment when catastrophe, real or imagined, threatens. The "end of Hong Kong," to reiterate an important point, is therefore what inaugurates an intense interest in its historical and cultural specificity, a change from the hitherto almost exclusive fascination with its economic success. This is very precisely a culture of disappearance because it is a culture whose appearance is accompanied by a sense of the imminence of its disappearance, and the cause of its emergence—1997—may also be the cause of its demise. The affective state of disappearance can be compared to that deliberately created by a cigarette company when it displayed in a public space in Hong Kong a sign that read, "No smoking. Not even Viceroy." In both cases, a negative situation, or one perceived as such, functions to provoke a desire for the quick fix of a smoke or of an identity. Such a concern for "Hong Kong culture" will indeed extend to an interest in its architecture and in the preservation of old buildings, but such an interest will have to be situated in turn within a space of disappearance.

A second sense of disappearance concerns representation. In disappearance there is a gap or *hysteresis* between the city and its representations, that is to say, between the city's erratic historical fortunes and the attempts to explain its itinerary in terms of available models like modernization, dependency, or development. The way the city has been made to appear in many representations in fact works to make it disappear. Let me offer two examples to illustrate this paradoxical relation between representation and disappearance, one positive and one negative.

Consider the representation of Hong Kong as an East-West city, mixing tradition and modernity like memory and desire. We see this idea enshrined in one of the most durable images of Hong Kong, which shows a Chinese junk in Victoria Harbor against a backdrop of tall modernistic buildings. This image has gone beyond kitsch and stereotype, being promoted to, and promoted as, an urban archetype. We see it not only reproduced on countless postcards, but a stylized red junk is also the chosen logo of the Hong Kong Tourist Association. Whether the image "misrepresents" Hong Kong or not (is Hong Kong really no more than the world's largest Chinatown?) is not the issue here. What is at issue is how an image of Hong Kong's architecture and urban space is used to support a narrative that implicitly attributes the colony's success to the smooth combination of British administration and Chinese entrepreneurship. Such a narrative also mobilizes ethnic and psychologistic assumptions that cannot bear scrutiny: the dogma that Hong Kong people are by nature hardworking, that they have a high tolerance for crowded living conditions by genetic design, that they will do anything for money. Peeping out from under this narrative is a master discourse that, seeing only its own mirror reflections, inscribes the primacy of the economic everywhere in the most literal-minded fashion. This is a discourse that elsewhere I have called decadent.[11] This discourse manages to make a complex space disappear into a one-dimensional image, structured on a facile binarism. Such a binarism not only tends to domesticate differences and restabilize change; it also avoids the spatial issues, to give us only a copulation of clichés (Vladimir Nabokov's excellent definition of pornography).

Consider now a negative representation of Hong Kong, the obvious one of the city as a colony and dependent territory of Britain. It is true that the recent British decision to issue passports only to a relatively small number of Hong Kong-British citizens giving them the right of abode in Britain clearly shows the small colonial mentality at work, but on the whole the effects of British colonialism on Hong Kong would seem on the surface to have been relatively benign. However, to say this is not by any means to whitewash the history of British imperialism or to forget the Opium Wars. If the British could point with some justification to a record of nonexploitation in Hong Kong, it would be largely because there was to begin with little of substance to exploit, neither natural resources nor, until after 1949 when the city was swelled by refugees from China, human resources. In these respects, the Hong Kong case is very different from that of British India, where colonialism effectively destroyed the local textile industry, a situation much easier to analyze in terms of dependency theory. As for Hong Kong, its very lack of resources or means of being independent was always curiously enough a factor in its favor: it meant that more could be gained all around by making the city work as a port city—by developing infrastructure, education, international networks. This was a position that both the colonizer and the colonized could agree on, a position of cute correspondence or collusion—hence the relative absence of political tensions or demands for "democracy," until recently. Again and again in the history of Hong Kong, we see how lack and dependency were somehow advantages. For example, when the colony went into textile manufacturing, it was able to develop an international market ahead of Taiwan or Korea because unlike these countries with their larger populations, Hong Kong lacked a significant domestic market.[12] The way ahead was never toward independence, but always toward hyperdependency. To call Hong Kong a colony is hardly a misrepresentation; it merely leaves out how dependency has been turned into a fine art.

These examples do not define at what point Hong Kong moved ahead of its cultural representations, but at least they tell us that for some time it has been somewhere other than where it is represented to be. Other cities like Los Angeles or Tokyo were built on seismic fault lines or volcanic soil:

Hong Kong seems to have been built on contingency, on geographic and historical accidents, shaped by times and circumstances beyond its control and by pragmatic accommodation to events. The harder we try to categorize it, the more the city mocks the available categories and remains, in spite of its overwhelming presence, a peculiar kind of "invisible city"—it appears in the moment of disappearance (first sense), and it disappears in appearances/representations (second sense).

Yet cutting across the ambivalences of appearance/disappearance is always a specific historical situation—how can it be otherwise?—and this suggests a third way in which a space of disappearance could be conceptualized: as a space that is historically produced. Yet to say this is not to imply that there is a historical narrative that, however it twists and turns, can nevertheless be definitive. A history of disappearance cannot but be inflected by the problematics of disappearance itself because if a space of disappearance can elude familiar representations, it can also elude historical descriptions. Hence the need to say something about the complex relation between space and history in Hong Kong, that is, to speak of spatial histories, not least because such histories will tend to modify some common assumptions about the forms that both colonialism and postcolonialism would take. As I have tried to show, the new Hong Kong cinema's ability to link history, space, and affectivity is what accounts for its privileged position.

A space of disappearance challenges historical representation in a special way, in that it is difficult to describe precisely because it can adapt so easily to any description. It is a space that engenders images so quickly that it becomes *nondescript*. For example, even a text as programmatically antirealistic and nonhistorical as Alain Robbe-Grillet's *La Maison de rendez-vous*, set tongue-in-cheek in Hong Kong, still captures *something* about the city's historical quality; it captures the way the nondescript heightens fantasy and gives rise to promiscuous images.[13] We can think about a nondescript space as that strange thing: an ordinary, everyday space that has somehow lost some of its usual systems of interconnectedness, a deregulated space. Such a space defeats description not because it is illegible and none of the categories fit, but because it is hyperlegible and all the categories seem to fit, whether they are the categories of the social sciences, of cultural criticism, or of fiction. Any description then that tries to capture the features of the city will have to be, to some extent at least, stretched between fact and fiction, somewhat like what we find in Jorge Luis Borges's short story *Emma Zunz*.[14] If this is the case, then there can be no single-minded pursuit of signs that finishes with a systematic reading of the city, only a compendium of *indices of disappearance* (like the nondescript) that takes into account the city's errancy and that addresses the city through its heterogeneity and parapraxias. A spatial history of disappearance will attempt to evoke the city rather than claim to represent it, in the sense of giving a definitive account of what it is "really" like.

Histories of Hong Kong tell a story of successful development, depicting the colony's gradual gains in material substance with an appeal to statistics. Conversely, some recent histories that are more politically conscious emphasize the colony's relative absence of democratic institutions and right to self-determination. Such stories, valid though they may be on one level, require some qualification because they leave out the way the colony's fortunes follow not just a logic of development or a logic of "oppression," but also a more paradoxical spatial logic where lack and dependency could somehow be advantageous. For example, statistics indeed show that at the last estimate Hong Kong is now the world's eighth-largest trading nation, an international city that has come a long way from the days when it was described in Palmerston's famous words as "a barren island with hardly a house upon it." But for all the discontinuities this new role implies, it has continued to be a *port* in the literal sense of the word: a door, a threshold, a conduit through which goods, currencies, and information flow; a kind of nodal point, an in-between state, therefore more of an inter-national city than an international one. It is true that the nature of the port or gateway has changed today: it connotes not just a good harbor but also an efficient communications system. The nature of the port may have changed, but Hong Kong has not changed as a port. In contrast to international cities like New York, London, or Toyko, which are in relation to their respective regions central sites for the production of goods and culture,[15] Hong Kong is primarily a space of facilitation. It is less a site than a *para-site*, in that its dominance in its region is due largely to its geographic proximity to China, together with its accessibility to the rest of the world. It is easy to see the economic opportunities that stem from being in such a unique geopolitical position. The para-site therefore connotes a position that in some strange way is both autonomous and dependent at the same time, a position in which autonomy is paradoxically a function of dependence.

In the inter-national city and the para-sitic city, something happens to the sense of time, of chronology. Consider once again how the space of Hong Kong has been formed: as a result not just of rapid changes but of an accelerated rate of change produced by historical events whose epicenters are elsewhere. Hong Kong by now has become so inured to change, to "progress," that it can be taken as the perfect example of the situation that Gianni Vattimo describes as the experience of "the end of history," a situation where "progress becomes routine," which does not imply that "progress" has been absorbed, much less understood.[16] Nevertheless, one crucial effect of such routinization is a weakening of the sense of chronology, of historical sequentiality, so that "old" and "new" are easily contemporaneous with each other, and "continuities" and "discontinuities" can exist side by side, *without being integrated.* Perhaps the most powerful symbolization of this is in cinema, particularly in Stanley Kwan's figure of the ghost in *Rouge* that returns after fifty years to seek her lover, a revenant stepping out of a freeze-frame. But other examples could be cited. For instance, it is not anomalous to see a high-rise building, including Norman Foster's Hong Kong Shanghai Bank building with its space-age materials, surrounded by the traditional Chinese bamboo scaffolding during construction—a kind of spatial palimpsest. A palimpsest of another sort was the fantastic sum of HK$9.5 million paid recently by a property developer for the "lucky" automobile license number "2": lucky because 2 in Chinese is a homonym of the word "easy" and because the number 2, shaped like a rooster (if we are willing to stretch our imaginations a bit), was purchased in the year of the rooster.[17] On one level, we can see this as simply old-fashioned superstition, a case of "numermancy" and a waste of money. But we could also see it, on another level, as money well spent in the purchase of what amounts almost to a company logo, a smart investment in the society of the spectacle. "Premodern" and "postmodern" join hands without having to acknowledge each other. Or take the example of built space. We have seen how high-investment buildings in Hong Kong are threatened by demolition, how what looks very permanent is in fact very temporary. But by the same logic, the temporary can also have a relative permanence. One example, by no means isolated, that comes to mind is a licensed food market in Western at the entrance of which is a sign that says "Smithfield Road Temporary Market." But the market has been there for as long as anyone can remember, and it seems to all intents and purposes very much like a permanent fixture of the neighborhood. What remains permanent, it seems, are places that are as yet unmarketable. These examples suggest that the space of Hong Kong is a space of "uneven development" in a specific sense: it is a space traversed by different times and speeds, where change has no clear direction but is experienced as a series of anticipations and residues that jostle each other for position. These are not examples of anachronisms, as anachronisms are perceived as chronology violated; rather, they are examples of what might be called *achronicities*, where past and present disappear in each other.

One main implication of the discussion so far is that disappearance pulls in different directions. It is heterogeneous and contradictory, not a seamless web. On the one hand, Hong Kong as a space of disappearance shows how the city dealt with dependency by developing a tendency toward timelessness (achronicity) and placelessness (the inter-national, the para-sitic), a tendency to live its own version of the "floating world" without the need to establish stable identities. On the other hand, disappearance also alludes to the new cultural mood that registers, with a high degree of urgency, the need to have some kind of cultural identity in place before Hong Kong reenters the Chinese fold. This confrontation with history within a space of disappearance will have an effect on how we look at Hong Kong's urban space and on what we understand by a Hong Kong architecture.

Ways of Seeing the City

Writing in the fifties, the Situationists already noted that "the visual aspect of cities counts only in relation to the psychological effects which it will be able to produce."[18] The remark itself can only have come out of a contemporary experience of the city. The movement away from the visual shows how problematic our visual experience of the city has become. Cities bombard us with a profusion of signs in various states of motion that distract and confuse, from traffic to advertisements to televisual media, all of which compete for attention with buildings. Hong Kong is said to have the largest Marlboro Man sign in the world, the size of a multistory building. Bilingual, neon-lit advertisement signs are not only almost everywhere; their often ingenious construction for maximum visibility deserves an architectural monograph in itself. The result of all this insistence is a turning off of the visual. As people in metropolitan centers tend to avoid eye contact with one another, so they now tend also to avoid eye contact with the city. When the visual becomes problematic because it is too complex, too conflicting, too unfamiliar, or too manipulative, then different ways of seeing the city—different scopic regimes—have to be brought into play.

We can relate the different ways of seeing the city to a typology of urban space recently proposed by Arata Isozaki and Akira Asada.[19] In their typology, Isozaki and Asada distinguish between three kinds of urban space, each defined according to an increasingly attenuated relationship to its historical context. Thus *real* cities are those that have preserved their historical contexts; *surreal* cities are metropolitan centers like Tokyo where urban elements are mixed up and hybridized without regard for historical context; and *hyperreal/simulated* cities are theme-park cities like Walt Disney World, devoid of context and based on fiction and artifice. We could now construct a typology of scopic regimes that would roughly correspond to Isozaki and Asada's urban typology: "real" cities encourage a regime of the visible or seen; "surreal" cities, a regime of the subliminal and uncanny or half-seen; "hyperreal" cities, a regime of the televisual or quickly seen. Both typologies and the relation between them become useful if we bear in mind that they give us only examples of "ideal types." Actual cities of a certain magnitude and complexity—like Tokyo or Hong Kong—tend to be a mixture of all three kinds outlined in Isozaki and Asada's typology: they are real, surreal, and hyperreal all at once and can be seen in different ways. This mixed nature of the metropolis is important because it means that *there is always a choice of scopic regimes available,* so that the choices that are actually made are historically significant. We can see now how these remarks might apply in the case of Hong Kong.

For better or for worse, it is almost impossible to get any sense of Hong Kong's urban space through the merely visible. Perhaps the only people who still "see" the city are the tourists. But then what is visible to them are only landmarks and monuments pointed out in guidebooks, while local history means only the exotic. The more "historical" a city, the more it falls prey to the tourist's gaze. As Henri Lefebvre reminds us, a purely visual space "has no social existence . . . that which is merely seen (and merely visible) is hard to see—but it is spoken of more and more eloquently and written of more and more copiously."[20] In this regard, it is interesting to note how a number of Hong Kong films made recently, which concern themselves with the city's present historical situation, attempt to identify the city by rendering it visible, particularly by shooting what is most visible of all, its architecture. These films range from Evans Chan's highly serious *To Liv(e)* to Tsui Hark's tongue-in-cheek *Wicked City*. But because architecture is seen as a purely photogenic set of objects, we get the same familiar shots of the same well-known buildings, taken from the same angles: looking down toward the harbor from the Peak, looking up toward the Peak from the harbor. It is as if it were necessary to hold on to the familiar for reassurance that the city is real. In any case, no identity emerges. Like a docile child, the city is seen but not heard.

Changing cities produce many sights that are unfamiliar. But rapidly changing cities, cities without brakes like Hong Kong, produce something else as well: *the unfamiliar in the familiar*, that is, the unfamiliar that is half-seen or seen subliminally behind the seen/scene of the familiar. This is the experience of the uncanny,[21] when the sense of "I am here," of the familiar and the homely shades into a sense of "I have been here before," of the *Unheimlich*, when what is seen is mixed up with a feeling of the already seen, of déjà vu. It was Louis Aragon, the surrealist poet, who captured the uncanny and subliminal nature of the rapidly changing city best, with its "disquieting atmosphere of places . . . peopled with unrecognized sphinxes." On the Paris arcades that were fast disappearing as a result of modern city planning, he wrote: "It is only today, when the pickaxe menaces them, that they have at last become the true sanctuaries of a cult of the ephemeral. . . . Places that were incomprehensible yesterday, and that tomorrow will never know."[22] The subliminal that Aragon evokes so well problematizes the visual, but it has not broken with it. That is why the subliminal is experienced in part visually, but also in part *allegorically*, that is, in terms of a spatio-temporal delay that prevents sign and meaning from coinciding. In allegory, signs are allowed their errancy; they become provocative: disquieting and sphinx-like, they provoke the making of narratives, including narratives of identity.

It would seem, therefore, that allegory is an appropriate mode for experiencing the peculiar realities of Hong Kong's urban space—except for one overriding consideration. As the city moves from manufacturing toward a greater concentration on service and finance, the regime of the televisual becomes increasingly dominant, introducing a new experience of space that Paul Virilio associates with what he calls the "tele-conquest of appearance." This televisual space is characterized by visual overload, the fusion and confusion of the fast and the slow, the absence of transition between the big and the small, the breakdown of the analogical in favor of the digital. The result is a "tele-observation in which the observer has no immediate contact with the observed reality."[23] The effect of the televisual is that it destroys allegory as defined, by the same process in which the delays of time and space are canceled out by the speed of electronic media. But in this regime of insistent and quick visibility, the unfamiliar is no longer a provocative dimension of the familiar. The unfamiliar, through instant replays and "real-time" transmissions, itself becomes all too familiar, and the strange madness of the déjà vu turns into the ordinary madness of the *déjà disparu*, as the regime of the televisual threatens to supplant all other ways of looking at the city.

The question is how to see the city? Which scopic regime should we choose? The choice is a difficult, if not impossible, one as none of the ways of seeing the city seems appropriate to the situation of present-day Hong Kong. If the tourist's gaze gives us ready-made images of the city that have no social substance, and if the allegorical gaze is destroyed by the televisual, then we are left with the latter, which serves only to promote a sense of placelessness. At one time, in the shadowless days before the anxieties of 1997 and Tiananmen, a sense of placelessness—which went together with an absence of strong local identities—was an asset, as it allowed Hong Kong to capitalize on its being a space-in-between. Now faced with the possibility of having an alien identity imposed on it from China— Hong Kong, British Dependent Territory may be as different from Xiang Gang China, as Paris, Texas is from Paris, France—there is immense pressure to develop an identity instantly. The danger, as I suggested earlier, is that in the representation of disappearance, even ersatz images may be found acceptable. It is at this juncture that the question what is Hong Kong architecture? becomes particularly relevant.

What Is Hong Kong Architecture?

If we take Hong Kong architecture at face value, we will see it merely as a sign of Hong Kong's growing prosperity. For example, even one otherwise astute commentator on Hong Kong could speak of the "flowering of architecture, art and culture" as "one more aspect of Hong Kong's financial success. . . . Certainly, the skyscrapers which have been put up in recent years have a reasonable number of architectural masterpieces among them. It is no longer necessary for Hong Kongers to feel that they live in a philistine city lacking in elegance."[24] Such a view, though meant to be laudatory, simply sees architecture as capitalism inscribed in built space. It is necessary therefore to stress, when we pose the question of Hong Kong architecture, that built space bears more than one inscription, that built space is overinscribed.[25] If there is a message, it is a jumbled one, not reducible to one meaning. In this regard, it is worth recalling Roland Barthes's remarks when, speculating on the possibilities of a nonreductive urban semiology, he referred to the city's "erotic dimension." However abstract it might seem, the city has a diversity that makes it potentially a space of pleasure and encounter, "the site of our encounter with the other."[26] The built space of the city not only evokes financial progress and the spatial appropriations of power but also gives us cultural residues, dreams of the future, as well as intimations of resistance. Built space therefore must not be understood only as spatial forms, but also as something that both produces and is produced by cultural practices. In the case of Hong Kong architecture, these will be the practices that relate to a culture of disappearance. We may begin by identifying three features.

The first concerns Hong Kong's receptivity to architectural styles. Architecture as buildings may always be situated in a place, but architecture as style and ideology is eminently transposable. In its architecture as in so much else, Hong Kong is an "open city," exposed to all styles and influences: from the vernacular to the colonial, from modernism to postmodernism. This extreme receptivity is unusual and could be related as much to its "floating" identity as to its growing affluence and accelerated development. In other words, space has as much to do with subjectivity as with economics. Many accounts of the city point out that Hong Kong does not look very different from other Asian cities, with its indiscriminate mix of drab and grandiose buildings. However, all we have to do is compare Hong Kong with a city like Taipei, which is quite as affluent, to see the difference. Taipei also displays a mixture of architectural styles, but the overall feeling is not quite the same. One of Taiwan's strongest claims to political legitimacy has always been to present itself as the true custodian of "Chinese culture." As a result, there is a kind of hesitancy in its employment of contemporary architectural forms, which stems from the implicit ideological interference of its image of Chinese identity. Hong Kong has neither a fixed identity nor the inhibitions that come from it. Hence the sharp contrast—to take one example—in the two cities' respective cultural centers. The Chiang Kai-shek cultural complex is a pastiche of Chinese architectural styles, while the Hong Kong cultural center is committed to contemporaneity.

Besides its receptivity to architectural styles, a second feature that is hard not to notice about Hong Kong is the constant building and rebuilding, which might remind us of that old joke about the colony: "A nice city—once it is finished." The building and rebuilding suggest that space is almost like a kind of very expensive magnetic tape that could be erased and reused. Here again, economic factors dovetail with subjective responses. What is erased are cultural memories; what is rebuilt are more profitable buildings. This applies to Hong Kong as a whole, but it is particularly true of Central, which is not only Hong Kong's business district today, but also the area that historically was the first to be developed. There are almost no vestiges of this past history in Central, except for the old colonial-style Supreme Court building, which has been preserved from the bulldozers and used now for Legislative Council meetings. In fact, one of the more paradoxical aspects of colonial space as a space of disappearance is the way in which "preservation" itself, as I have suggested earlier, could be part of the process of this erasure of cultural memories.

But perhaps the most noticeable feature of all is the city's hyperdensity, estimated at more than forty thousand people per square mile. Even this high figure is only an overall average; there are indeed many areas like Mongkok and Shumshuipo that have considerably higher densities, or the recently demolished Walled City, which with an area of one-hundredth of a square mile had a population of thirty-three thousand, giving it a density of more than three million per square mile, by far the highest in the world. Building expanded in two directions: horizontally, following the flat land along the coastline and areas reclaimed from the sea; vertically, in the form of high-rises that are like new kinds of walled cities. Finally, because high-density space has to serve a variety of purposes, form does not necessarily follow function, and there is in most districts no neat separation of commercial from residential use. I shall come back to this question of hyperdensity in a moment.

These features—heightened receptivity to stylistic influences, constant rebuilding, hyperdensity—do not in themselves define Hong Kong architecture for us. However, what the thematics of susceptibility to influence and the erasure of cultural memory suggest is that the question of Hong Kong architecture is intimately related to the question of Hong Kong's cultural self-definition, which in a space of disappearance can only be problematic. I propose, therefore, to approach Hong Kong architecture indirectly by considering different kinds of built space in the city and the urban issues they raise: issues about preservation and memory, about political allegory, about subjectivity.

A full survey of Hong Kong architecture will have to use many different categories and include the discussion of many different architectural examples. For the present purpose, however, we can divide Hong Kong's built space into three main types. Each type can claim to represent some aspect of Hong Kong, and in this sense to be regarded as "local"—which merely serves to show how difficult it is to locate the local. On the one hand, there is what I will call the *Merely Local,* which consists of all those buildings largely belonging to another historical era, existing now, if they exist at all, mainly on the economic margins of the city. These include the indigenous architecture that has roots in the Qing dynasty; the buildings in the urban vernacular style resembling that in Guangzhou and Shanghai; and the colonial-style constructions found also in Malaysia and India,[27] one gracious example of which is the Main Building of the University of Hong Kong. On the other hand, we have the *Placeless*, all those impressive multinational hotels and office buildings with no local memories, concentrated mainly in Central but now also moving eastward toward the reclaimed land north of Gloucester Road on harborside Wanchai. These buildings could be found almost anywhere in the world, and they seem to have just *landed* on their sites out of nowhere. In between the Merely Local and the Placeless, acting somewhat like a buffer zone, is the *Anonymous*, all those nondescript commercial and residential blocks that seem to replicate themselves endlessly. These buildings may not inspire a second look, but they constitute the majority of built space in Hong Kong.

The Merely Local have a close link with Hong Kong's history and topography. Besides temples and shrines, they include those dwellings built on water that remind us that Hong Kong was once a fishing village. One example would be the sampan boats adapted as live work space still found in Aberdeen and Causeway Bay. However, the number of sampans is now dwindling, as more of the (literally) floating population is "repatriated" to dry land to look for more conventional work and more conventional living space. Another example are the houses built on stilts near the sea, still found, for example, in the fishing village of Tai O to the northwest of Lantau Island. This once thriving village is now getting quite run-down, turned into a receiving center for smuggled goods; its main product, a preserved salted fish, is an ironic emblem of the village itself. In the New Territories can be found a number of villages of another kind, the indigenous Chinese-style walled village. One example is the Tsang Tai Uk in Shatin, still inhabited, and coexisting as in a time warp with and within sight of the government public housing blocks close by. The urban-vernacular-style buildings have largely gone except for a few scattered examples in Western, but a number of colonial-style structures can still be seen, like the previously discussed Flagstaff House and a much-gentrified Western Market, which has been turned into a kind of museum/mall on the model of Covent Garden and which now houses a number of Chinese restaurants and boutiques.

The Merely Local may have been structures rooted in a time and place, but it is a time and place that is no longer there. These structures may have interesting stories to tell, but they have no real voice in the present-day life of the city, which has moved elsewhere. However, they do raise an important and difficult issue about cultural memory and preservation, particularly about the difference between them. While one could certainly accept the rationale of preserving old buildings as a counterweight to the placelessness and anonymity of the rest of the city, there is in present-day Hong Kong another factor to consider: the way the impetus to preservation partly arises, as I suggested earlier, out of the ambivalences of a culture of disappearance. Even in more straightforward colonial situations like the ones analyzed by Anthony King, preservation is marked by ambiguity. For example, King describes what he calls "the 'preservation' syndrome": "In the colonial context, this has a double irony. Not only does planning effort go into inculcating the colonized culture with similar values but the criteria of the colonial power are used to define and 'preserve' 'buildings of architectural and historic importance,' while remnants of the indigenous culture are left to disappear."[28] In any case, preservation is not the same as memory: it is a memory without pain. In preserving what was there, there is a danger of blotting out of memory *what was not there*, which is just as important. Preservation in its selectiveness is the disappearance of memory, and this dis-appearance, like the kinds of representation discussed earlier, can be very significant politically at this particular juncture of Hong Kong's history. It is surely not accidental that so many of the examples of preservation end up implicitly giving us history as decoration, as nostalgia. Nostalgia, we can say, is not the return of past memory: it is the return of memory to the past. Nostalgia is déjà vu without the uncanny.

In sharp contrast to the Merely Local are those Placeless international buildings that usually get the most attention. They are buildings that are meant to be *read*, and according to Henri Lefebvre, such spaces made to be read are

> the most deceptive and tricked up imaginable. . . . Monumentality, for instance, always embodies and imposes a clearly intelligible message. . . . monumental buildings mask the will to power and the arbitrariness of power beneath signs and surfaces which claim to express collective will and collective thought. In the process, such signs and surfaces also manage to conjure away both possibility and time.[29]

More and more, monumental buildings are no longer only found in Central. The newest one, cheekily calling itself Central Plaza, is located in Wanchai and is now (but not for long) the tallest building in Asia. The Placeless do not look local, but they are highly vocal. They do not so much tell a story as make a point, a rhetorical, usually phallocentric point: I am the tallest or the smartest or the most contemporary or the most expensive. Exchange Square, which houses the Hong Kong Stock Exchange and the offices of major international banks, used to be one of the smartest buildings around; nowadays, it is getting stiff competition from new arrivals like the Citibank Plaza in Central. The China Bank was Hong Kong's tallest building when it was built; now that title goes to Central Plaza, although the bank can still think of itself as being more elegant. The recently completed Number 9 Queen's Road was perhaps the first building in Hong Kong to pride itself on being "postmodern," and hence very "contemporary," because it played with architectural period styles. The most expensive and technologically advanced is still the Hong Kong Bank. And so it goes. All this architectural rhetoric seemed ripe for deconstruction. When Zaha Hadid took part in an international competition to build a luxury club in Hong Kong's Peak area, she produced a design that was quite antirhetorical. One chief feature of the design consisted of having four huge beams laid flat and driven into the hillside—an image of horizontally embedded "skyscrapers" to deconstruct the general rhetoric of verticality and phallocentrism.[30]

The two most impressive buildings in Hong Kong are still the two banks, the Hong Kong Shanghai Bank built by the British architect Norman Foster and the Bank of China Tower by the overseas Chinese architect I. M. Pei. It is possible to see a political allegory emerging as we watch these two buildings stand in all their monumentalism close to each other in Central, locked in a relation of spatial and political rivalry, even if it is an allegory of disappearance, as we shall see presently. The Foster building is reputed to be the world's most expensive piece of real estate. Constructed of space-age materials by a multinational team, its form is a brash celebration of high technology. By contrast, the more elegant Pei building is a kind of architectural ode to verticality and visuality. Its basic geometric form is that of the prism: from an arrangement of four prisms that form the solid lower sections, it rises, twisting and becoming more ethereal, in successive arrangements of three, two, and finally a single prism that forms its topmost stories, the whole structure surmounted by two poles pointing it still further upward: I like to think of it as the *Toblerone* building, after the distinctively shaped Swiss chocolate bar. To what extent, we might ask, do these two buildings connote "China" and "Britain" in Hong Kong, and, on that basis, solicit the loyalties of its citizenry? The interesting point to note is that however different the architectural rhetoric of these two buildings may be, both can be regarded as simply examples of contemporary architecture, two variations within a single system. That may be why in an attempt at "localization" we see both buildings as incorporating design elements that have little to do with the formal logic of their structure. For example, the Hong Kong Shanghai Bank has retained as a kind of historical relic the two bronze lions that used to guard the entrance to the old bank building, two fierce lions of British imperialism. The problem, however, is that in the new building, there is no formal entrance as such, the ground floor now flowing into the roads on both sides, so that these two deterritorialized lions now look like harmless pussycats. In a similar effort at localization, the lower part of the otherwise unornamented glass-and-steel Pei building is decorated with black-and-white marble to give it a quasi-Chinese effect, while its twisting glass structure is often compared—with considerable contrivance—to bamboo. However, these efforts at differentiation only feebly disguise the fact that the spatial logic of these two buildings belongs to the same internationalist architectural system. This should force us to rethink the often repeated formula of "one country, two systems" as the political model for Hong Kong after 1997, the view of a future Hong Kong as a special capitalist enclave within a socialist country. What the city's built forms themselves tell us is the very different story of "one system" (that of international capital) at different stages of development. We find here a double set of disappearances, an allegory of disappearance, where the coziness implied by the phrase "one country" disappears in the global economic system, and, by the same token, where the idea of ideologically differentiated socioeconomic systems disappears as well.

In contrast to the architectural showpieces, the majority of the commercial and residential buildings in Hong Kong are not distinguished in any way. We find the same standardized forms replicating themselves whenever there is a site available. The huge residential estates, whether built by the government as public housing or by private enterprise, are like so many vertical walled villages. The result is that the present-day form of the urban vernacular presents us with a visual anonymity that spreads to most parts of the city and deprives it of architectural character. Yet for a number of reasons, the Anonymous may be the most articulate and significant of all.

To begin with, there is a relation between architectural anonymity and the question of hyperdensity. It could be argued that the only solution to the problem of hyperdensity was the instant high-rise and the enormous estate block. For example, the story is often told about Hong Kong's first housing estate at Shek Kip Mei, which was built very quickly in 1953 to house the thirty-three thousand people—mainly refugees from China—who were made homeless by a disastrous fire. Units in the estate—the Mark I model—were very basic, but it was at least an improvement on the shantytown-like conditions in which the inhabitants of Shek Kip Mei were living before. At present, 2.8 million people (about 50 percent of the population) live in government-subsidized housing, and the authorities are building forty thousand new flats a year to meet the demand. For a city with a reputation for social ruthlessness, these are surprising and praiseworthy figures that present us with a conundrum—until we realize, as a number of critics have pointed out, that the government's motivation for building these resettlement estates did not come entirely out of a concern for social welfare. Resettlement was a means of acquiring valuable development land; cheap housing reduced upward pressure on wages, thus allowing for the reproduction of cheap labor power, and it preempted and defused squatters' resistance to clearance.[31]

There is yet another (though related) side to the story. Hyperdensity is partly the result of limited space, but it is also a result of how this limited space could be exploited for economic gain. On the one hand, the colonial government deals with the problem of hyperdensity by constructing cheap housing estates. On the other hand, the government policy of releasing crown land bit by bit at strategic moments and its prerogative, which it duly exercises, of designating land as rural (where strict building restrictions apply) or urban, ensure that building space remains scarce and property prices remain high.[32] Complementing this is the banks' policy of giving preferential mortgage conditions to clients purchasing property less than ten years old and refusing to extend mortgages to property more than thirty years old, which means that developers are encouraged to build new properties, creating once more a demand for land. The anonymous highrise block, both public and private, must therefore be seen not simply as a necessary solution to the problem of hyperdensity; it is also a way of turning the problem to the owner's advantage and exists as an index of the problem. As long as this is the case, the urban vernacular will retain its one-dimensional character.

In the face of the Placeless landscape of power and the Anonymous urban vernacular, we might ask where, then, are the erotic spaces of pleasure and encounter, the heterotopic spaces of contestation, the liminal spaces of transition and change? There are not many examples that come to mind, and even those that do are somewhat ambiguous. Take the area around Statue Square on Sundays. The square is a small and not particularly attractive concrete park in Central, opposite the Hong Kong Bank and adjacent to the world-class Mandarin Hotel. It is one of the few open spaces in an intensely built-up area. On weekdays, Central is Hong Kong's no-nonsense business district, but on Sundays the migrant domestic workers from the Philippines, almost entirely female, congregate around the square, taking it over and turning it into something like a festive space. There they chat, exchange news and information, share a meal or a hometown newspaper. Some small-scale entrepreneurial activities also take place: there are part-time beauticians and manicurists, vendors of magazines in Tagalog, and so on. At one time, the authorities made some halfhearted attempts at discouraging these weekly meetings, but now they have made the area into a traffic-free zone on weekends. Is Statue Square on Sundays an example then of the *détournement* or diversion of a space of power into a space of pleasure? This is unfortunately not entirely the case because the weekly congregations take place only by permission, and come Monday everything returns to "normal." No contestation has taken place. Perhaps the takeover of Central is more clearly an example of the fascination that the symbolic spaces of power exert on those excluded from them. The powerless are allowed to see Central—like looking at so many goods through a shop window—but not to touch it.

A somewhat different example is the area that takes its name after an old street in Central, Lan Kwei Fong. The area is situated in the hilly and less accessible part of Central, which therefore made it much less prestigious and desirable as commercial space. Not too long ago, Lan Kwei Fong was just an unremarkable and unfashionable bit of space on the commercial periphery, with its narrow streets, little shops and low-grade offices, local restaurants, flower stalls and street cobblers. It was just part of Hong Kong's anonymous urban vernacular. But as even this description already suggests, the area has its picturesque aspects that could be turned to advantage; it could be gentrified, as some business minds began to see. A string of smart restaurants began to appear, followed by European-style beer halls serving special brews, coffee bars, Hong Kong's only jazz club, art galleries, and generally stylish meeting places. The flower stalls and street cobblers are still there, next to high-tech chrome and Plexiglass shop fronts. The streets themselves have been repaved with cobblestones to give them a certain "Ye Olde" look. The atmosphere is American (particularly Californian), European, and local all at the same time. This cheekily mixed space makes the area instantly appealing to those who like to think of themselves as hip and arty; it certainly appeals to the young and affluent, the upwardly mobile who do not mind the hilly location and the steep prices. However, as a space of pleasure and encounter, which it clearly is, Lan Kwei Fong has one major drawback: the high cost of admission, although teenagers can and do stroll around its streets for free. Lan Kwei Fong may have some of the appearance of a liminal space, but it turns out to be just a variant of the dominant theme of capital. To use Sharon Zukin's terms, the plain "vernacular" is appropriated by capital and transformed into desirable "landscape."[33] But this process of transformation is entirely determined by commercialism and is ultimately indifferent to the urban vernacular at large, which remains untransformed by this example. In this regard, the space of Lan Kwei Fong can be compared to that of the more recently built mall-and-entertainment complex that calls itself Times Square, although the two look very different. Times Square, situated between Causeway Bay and Happy Valley on Russell Street, which was once a local market street, was designed as an autonomous inner-looking space, indifferent to its surroundings (like the "postmodern" spaces Fredric Jameson has described). Thus visitors to the mall can ride up and down on its glass-cased elevators and, protected by the mall itself, look out with a certain pleasure straight into the interiors and rooftops of the run-down apartment houses just a few meters away on the other side of Russell Street. Lan Kwei Fong displays a comparable spatial indifference. It is a much-appropriated vernacular space that has forgotten that it is vernacular.

The third example takes us back to the question of the vernacular response to the problem of hyperdensity. A team of Japanese architects who recently did a study of Hong Kong's urban space focused precisely on this issue of hyperdensity and came up with some surprising conclusions.[34] They began by contrasting two ways of dealing with it. One way is suggested by modernist ideas of town planning derived from Le Corbusier's vision of the "contemporary City for 3 million people," which put the stress on a separation of functions, a segregation of commercial and residential spaces. But would separation lead to the mutual enhancement of these spaces, or to the creation of a boring homogeneity? The other way is that of "Hong Kong, the Alternative Metropolis," which consists of aggressively mixing up the functions, of not rigidly separating public and private, commercial and residential space. The result, it is argued, is heterogeneity, vitality, complexity. For example, Hong Kong may be one of the few cities in the world where one finds people in pyjamas strolling in shopping malls. Even when ideas are taken over from modernist town planning, they are changed in the process. Take the idea of the pedestrian walkway, whose rationale was to separate automobiles from people. We find a system of walkways in Central and in some of the new towns, but their function is changed. In Central, for example, walkways do not separate people from cars: they simply provide an additional or alternative path, while in the new towns themselves we often find walkways lined with shops and boutiques. The tendency then is not toward specialization and separation, but toward the multiplication and concentration of different functions in the same space. But perhaps the most characteristic way of all of dealing with hyperdensity is to transform the facades of anonymous apartment blocks by the construction of illegal and semilegal structures: balconies, indoor gardens, additional storage space, and so on. It is as if the flat surfaces of these anonymous buildings were now covered in pleats or folds, multiplying in volume and interest and providing a zone of mediation between inside and outside.

In the argument of these Japanese architects, hyperdensity becomes positive, as anonymity is transformed into something that almost gives us the aesthetic pleasures of a baroque space, even if it is baroque by necessity rather than by design.[35] Diversity, too, reappears, not in terms of a profusion of architectural styles but in the internal modification of standardized forms, comparable perhaps to the new Hong Kong cinema's use of genre. Such an argument, attractive and hopeful though it is in some respects, nevertheless contains one serious flaw. It largely ignores the politics and economics of hyperdensity discussed earlier and accepts the proliferation of anonymous high-rise blocks as the only solution. The question then understandably becomes how to deal with this anonymity, for which they came up with a very elegant answer: make the vernacular baroque. But the very attractiveness of such an analysis of Hong Kong's urban space would only serve to ensure that no more radical transformation of the vernacular need take place.

When we reflect on these and other examples, it is hard to avoid the conclusion that Hong Kong architecture is not in quite the same sanguine position as the new Hong Kong cinema. The new cinema has found a subject: it has found Hong Kong itself as a subject, problematic and threatened by disappearance as that may be. As for Hong Kong architecture, it does not concern itself as yet with the question of cultural self-definition and presents to itself only the false image of power. As a result, the more Placeless and powerful buildings that get built, the more the urban vernacular remains anonymous and characterless. It should be emphasized, too, that anonymity is not only the result of hyperdensity; it is also a result of the too-easy receptivity to influence going together with the neglect of cultural memory. On the other hand, if anonymity could be overcome and some kind of identity established, it would most likely be of a paradoxical kind. It would not be identity as the establishment of something fixed and clearly defined, or as a return to something that was once there in the past. Rather, it would have to be identity as some form of hyphenation, coming into existence sometime in the future. Otherwise, it would be hard to answer the question of whether this future extends beyond 1997. To paraphrase Walter Benjamin, architecture would be in ruins even when—especially when—the monuments that make it up have not crumbled.

5

Photographing Disappearance

Hong Kong is one of the world's most photographed cities.

It is not a matter of producing more or better photographs of Hong Kong, but of using the photograph as a means of seeing what is involved in looking at and thinking about the city.

From this point of view, the project of photographing Hong Kong—photographing disappearance—is related to the project of a Hong Kong cinema and a Hong Kong architecture.

The camera lens puts the city on the couch. The visual is a means of interrogating visuality: its puns and parapraxia. Not just an optical unconscious; a spatial unconscious as well.

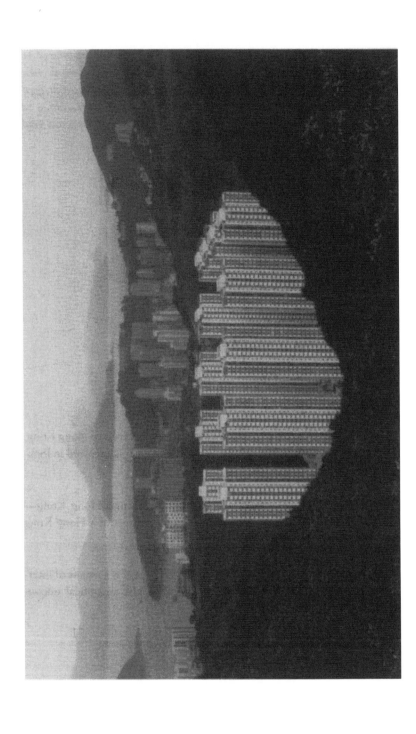

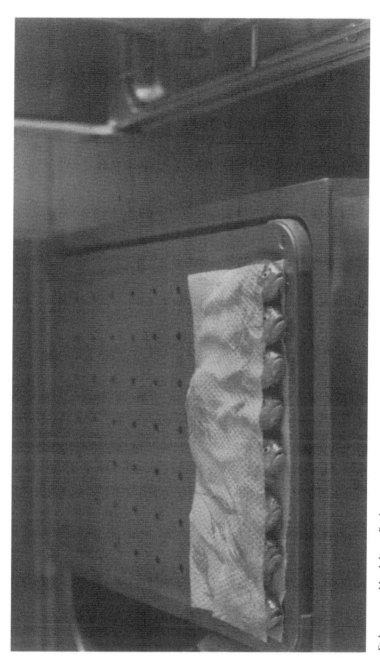

Fish arranged by Juliette Borbe

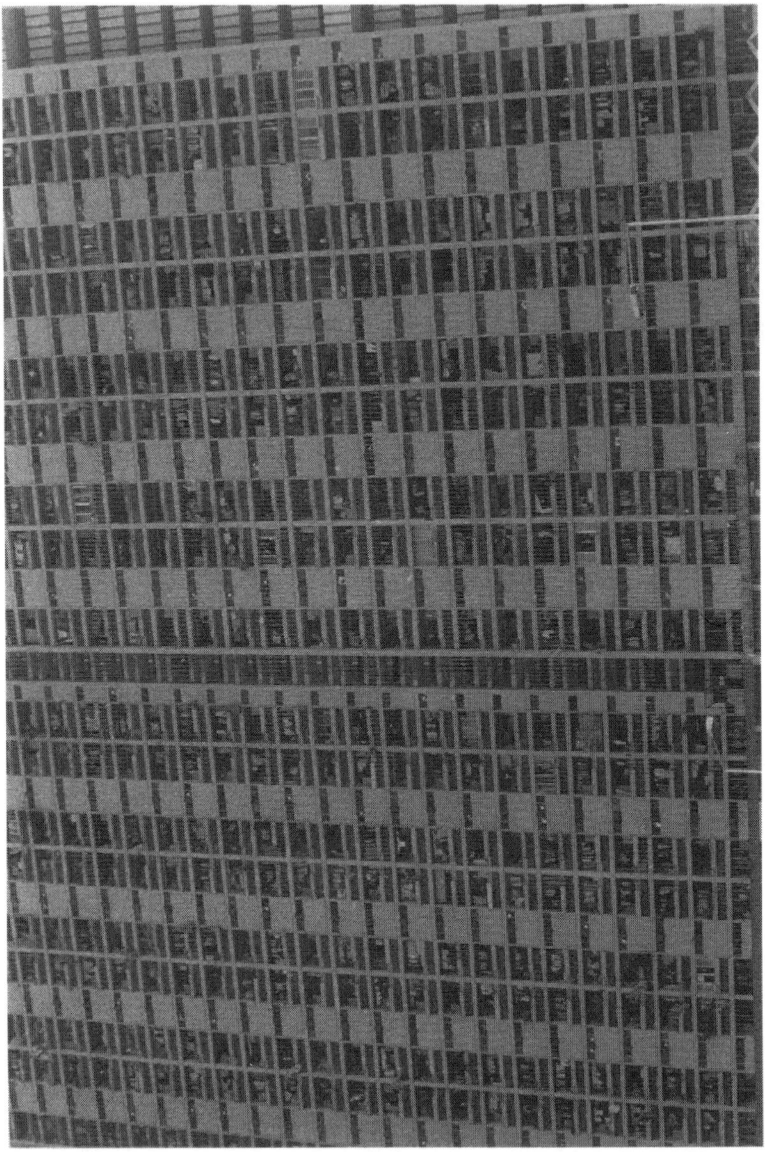

In picture postcards of Hong Kong, the implied referent is always "Hong Kong-ness." Hence the need to catch some representative and recognizable aspect of the city. A list of postcard subjects/themes would include:

The Celebration of Power—shots of the Hong Kong skyline, gravitating toward the landscape of power of Central; an emphasis on landmarks.

Stereotypes of Otherness—shots of sailing junks, rickshaws, the Peak tram, and other passé objects, that is, all those images that build up a picture of a mythic/exotic city, where "contrasts" are all too predictable and ethnic/cultural "mixtures" are made up of elements that are easily separable.

Hong Kong Graffiti—nostalgic images of old Hong Kong; not the return of past memory, but the return of memory to the past.

"What a Beautiful World"—"photography is unable to say anything about a power station or a cable factory other than this: what a beautiful world. . . . for it has succeeded in transforming even abject poverty, by recording it in a fashionably perfected manner, into an object of enjoyment." (Walter Benjamin) Case in point: photographs of the Kowloon Walled City.

The "ordinary" photograph differs in many respects from the picture postcard.

It does not claim to be representative, celebratory, expressive, or even critical. The referent is not assumed to be known. There is neither the shock nor the reassurance of recognition.

As document, it does not make evident; it provides evidence. As documentary, it puts the stress not on getting a fix on the object, but on chance, nonvoluntarism, opening the image to speculation.

It takes to heart Italo Calvino's description of cities: "With cities, it is as with dreams. . . . but even the most unexpected dream is a rebus that conceals a desire or, its reverse, a fear." It does not catch the city at a critical moment; it catches the city *out* at a moment of unawareness.

It encourages the viewer not so much to look—what is there to see?—as to *look again;* not so much to take in what is there, as to do a double take.

The sight of the city—what is given to view—is qualified by the site of the city, by the paradoxical nature of a cultural space of disappearance that challenges visual recuperation.

Roland Barthes believed that the photograph is always "a certificate of presence." Disappearance, too, is more a matter of presence rather than absence, of superimposition rather than erasure. Hence an elective affinity between the photograph and disappearance?

Photographing disappearance produces a thereness that is not quite there, a "concrete abstraction" (Henri Lefebvre).

It is not a question of empty lots and blurred images. Disappearance gives us not the poignancy of the ephemeral ("borrowed time, borrowed place") nor the pathos of the diasporic, but the paradox of a space we have to second guess in order to experience. A flat montage of "lost dimensions" (Paul Virilio).

To photograph disappearance is not to defamiliarize, only that a sense of the unfamiliar grows out of forms that remain stubbornly familiar. Like the uncanny.

To look out for indices of disappearance is not the same as to fetishize, or to seize on a detail as a substitute gratification faute de mieux; rather, it is a matter of interrogating in detail the fetish itself.

If the traumatic image is the image about which there is nothing to say (Barthes again), then nothing is more traumatic than the nondescript.

Like the uncanny, disappearance dissolves boundaries and moves toward the paradoxes of hyphenation, for example, "one country, two systems."

Hyphenation suggests a twist in cultural space. What separates also connects.

Hyphenation means that the photograph has to become comparative, in a situation where stable terms of comparison do not exist.

The release of the shutter, like a throw of the dice, can never abolish chance. Photographic seeing includes seeing the photograph as an object lesson in disappearance.

6

Writing Hong Kong

To speak of "Writing Hong Kong" implies something different from speaking of "Hong Kong Writing," even though it may sometimes be difficult to distinguish between them in any clear-cut way. The latter might involve embarking on a critical survey of local authors and of texts produced in and on Hong Kong. It would be concerned with discussing a wide and representative number of works, written mainly in Cantonese, that would define a corpus and lead to the establishment of a tradition of Hong Kong literature. It might even pose questions of identity like, what is a Hong Kong writer? or what constitutes an authentic Hong Kong text? By contrast, writing Hong Kong has a different emphasis. It is less concerned with authors and writing, or with problems of corpus formation, than with asking how in the process of writing Hong Kong, Hong Kong as cultural space inscribes itself in the text. It is concerned then with writing that bears the traces of such a cultural space (of disappearance). Such an emphasis has the advantage, at least for my purposes, of placing writing on the same footing as cinema and architecture vis-à-vis Hong Kong culture. This allows us to pose a number of questions that have been explored in previous chapters: questions of history, space and place, affectivity, language, the changing meaning of the local, and so on. But it would also allow us to pose these questions from the different angle of writing, and to raise some other questions as well.

We can use the notion of writing marked by a cultural space as a working principle of inclusion and exclusion. Such a discussion would include, for example, texts originally written not only in Chinese but also in English. Thus the poems in English by someone like Louise Ho could be included as a valid instance of writing Hong Kong. It would include texts that are not examples of what is conventionally understood to be "literature," like journalism, polemical essays, or travel notes. The pieces on Hong Kong by Lu Xun who is not a Hong Kong writer could be taken as examples of writing Hong Kong because, although they are "occasional" pieces, they nevertheless raise some of the finer issues involved in writing in and about the problematic cultural space of Hong Kong. On the other hand, it would exclude what in some ways is a fine and informative piece of writing, Jan Morris's book on Hong Kong, which does not raise these issues. It would clearly exclude novels like James Clavell's *Taipan* and *Noble House*, Robert Elegant's *Dynasty*, or Richard Mason's *The World of Suzie Wong*, all best-sellers that use Hong Kong basically as a setting against which a number of colonial and sexual fantasies unfold. These novels with their often thick and spectacular plots that glamorize the workings of capital all lack one characteristic: they cannot take the risk of addressing the ordinary and the banal, that is, of addressing the local, which is one of the most distinctive signs of writing Hong Kong.

Lu Xun and Sir Cecil Clementi

One of the key issues raised by writing Hong Kong is that of translation, particularly cultural translation. We can begin by reconstructing a confrontation between Lu Xun and Sir Cecil Clementi, one of the most distinguished governors of Hong Kong, a confrontation that never actually took place, but whose implications are still with us today.

In early 1927, Lu Xun was in Hong Kong for the first time on a lecture tour. He wrote two essays soon afterward about his Hong Kong experience. The second essay, about his being searched by Hong Kong customs officers, the theme of which is the corruption of the colonial mentality, is the better known one. But the first essay titled "On Hong Kong" is more interesting and particularly relevant to our discussion.[1] It not only displays Lu Xun's remarkable powers of observation; it also shows his understanding of the close relationship between culture, politics, and everyday life—his sense that both culture and politics can be located in apparently trivial events. Thus in Hong Kong Lu Xun reads the newspapers and picks up cultural contradictions everywhere. One of the most effective devices in his essay is direct quotation, which is a way of letting the evidence speak for itself. Take the following news item that Lu Xun picks out:

> Later last night, two men in suits . . . were searched by a British police officer at Shek Tong Tsui. One of the men spoke in English to the officer, but the latter ignored him and warned him by saying ***. Finally they ended up at the police station.

It is those ***'s representing what has been expurgated from the news report that arouses Lu Xun's curiosity: "Perhaps there's something fishy going on here. . . . The three ***'s seem to have been a result of the suits the men wore and the English they spoke. The British officer hated these two things; the language and dress belong only to the master race."

We might note that in writing about Hong Kong Lu Xun, like many mainland speakers of Mandarin, is not entirely free of a touch of linguistic imperialism toward a Cantonese-speaking city, admitting (with some pride) to not entirely understanding its "language." But on the whole, Lu Xun's essay, with its complex ironies, brings into sharp focus some of the cultural contradictions of Hong Kong society that are still with us today. We might go even further and say that it is not only a piece *about* Hong Kong; it can also be taken as one model of how the often confusing reality of this place can be represented—by passionate irony, by the relentless interrogation of local forms and practices, by the juxtaposition of incongruities. I will be coming back presently to the question of Lu Xun as a model for writing Hong Kong.

One of the items that Lu Xun is most ironic about in his essay is the text of a speech "in the Cantonese dialect" by a "Governor Jin," advocating what must look like an unexceptionable argument in the Hong Kong context: the importance of studying Chinese culture as a bridge between China and the West. Now this Governor Jin is none other than Sir Cecil Clementi, governor of Hong Kong from 1925 to 1930, and the argument looks that much more unexceptionable coming as it does from a Westerner. As Hong Kong governors go, Clementi was not only quite intellectually distinguished, a scholar and a thinker, as his speech, which Lu Xun quotes in its entirety, shows; he was also deeply concerned about social relations in the colony, as some of his other writings could testify:

> My acquaintance with Hong Kong and with things Chinese now extends over a quarter of a century and nothing has been a cause to me of more anxiety throughout that period than the fact that the Chinese and European communities of Hong Kong, although in daily contact with each other,

nevertheless move in different worlds, neither having any real comprehension of the mode of life or ways of thought of the other. This is a most regrettable misunderstanding which retards the social, moral, intellectual and even the commercial and material progress of the colony.[2]

Here we have that rare person (Sir David Wilson, governor from 1987 to 1992, is the only other example that comes to mind): a colonial administrator who knows Cantonese, the local language, and is interested enough in the local culture to translate some of its texts. We still have some of Clementi's translations, among which is a set of love songs translated from the Cantonese. I quote here a few representative lines:

> Each soul has its sorrow: this ye ought to quit and cast aside.
> The soul's sorrow galls: quit it, then there is peace.
> Wide, wide is the sea of bitterness: ill-fated be more than half therein:
> But whoso find joy amid the bitter, theirs is an angel-spirit.[3]

As we can see, Clementi's literary language unfortunately has not worn well. His translation follows the Cantonese original, yet the anonymous Cantonese poet comes across in it bathetically dressed in English coattails, for example, as seen in the stilted "ye" and "therein," and "whoso" and in the whole soppy fin de siècle Weltschmerz that is paraded in the movement of the syntax. Clementi's translation is instructive in that it shows how scholarship and good intentions are sometimes not enough. Meanwhile, let us examine the nature of Lu Xun's criticism.

Lu Xun prefaced his discussion of Clementi's speech with the sardonic remark that he thought it was given by "one of the die-hard adherents of the Qing dynasty whose articles all sound the same," and we will gradually see the force of this remark. He continues by noting that Clementi concludes his speech in defense of Chinese culture by using as a motto what he calls "four very inspiring lines" from the great classical literary anthology Wenxuan:

> To express our nostalgia for the past
> And meditate upon ancient days
> Carry forward the divine spirit of our ancestors
> Strike up the heavenly voice of Han grandeur.

On the face of it, these lines seem appropriate enough for Clementi's purpose—except for one important context that casts a different light on them. It is precisely these lines, Lu Xun points out, that revolutionary students at the end of the Qing dynasty used in their struggle against Manchu rule. When the students quoted these lines, it

> was supposed to remind us of the former greatness of the Han people and allow us to make a comparison with the present: we must recover our ancient treasures. Or to put it more explicitly, the idea was to "expel the Manchus," and by extension, "expel the foreigners." But twenty years after this was published, it has become a slogan for Hong Kong University's attempt to preserve Chinese culture and make "the relationship between China and the West grow closer and more friendly." It's hard to imagine these four lines from *Wenxuan* being quoted by a foreigner.

In using these historically loaded lines as exhortation to the study of Chinese culture, Clementi commits a literary malapropism that is also a political parapraxis, a mistake made possible perhaps by ignorance or by a "forgetting" of the ironic historical parallels between Manchu rule in China and British rule in Hong Kong; hence Lu Xun's sardonic prefatory reference to "die-hard adherents of the Qing dynasty." Elsewhere in the essay, Lu Xun also could not resist slipping in the remark, "it seems as if the British are eager students of the Chinese classics and of history." We might mention here in passing another instance of historical irony. When Hong Kong University's department of Chinese introduces the work of the department, it still quotes with approval lines from Clementi's now-famous speech, as if Lu Xun had not critiqued them. We can only speculate on what he would have said.

This "confrontation" between Lu Xun and Clementi is significant because it is also a confrontation between two notions of culture. As a colonial administrator with some literary talent, Clementi presents culture as something conciliatory, whose function it is to establish continuities and stability and to promote "East-West" understanding. But it is clear that the condition of such understanding is the expurgation to some extent from cultural texts of some of the elements of contestation and danger. Nowhere in Clementi's translations nor in his speech is there any hint as to the problematic space in which these texts are held. In this regard, the malaprop quotation goes together with the unfortunate bathetic note in his translations. They belong to an order of sensibility that assigns to culture the task of preservation, not the task of memory; culture as contributing to the obliteration and not the understanding of contradiction; culture as compensation or substitute for the messiness of history, as in the case of Flagstaff House discussed earlier, which uses a former British military base as a museum of Chinese teaware. For all his concern to keep the "different worlds" of Hong Kong in touch, Clementi seems curiously out of touch. In all these respects, Lu Xun comes across as the much more attractive and lively of the two in that he espouses a view of culture that sees it as open to change and transformation rather than as so many static monuments. Hence, in spite of his lack of intimacy with Hong Kong in 1927, his acerbic essay, more so than Clementi's well-intentioned speech or translations, is a more exciting example of writing Hong Kong.

Nevertheless, there is one other issue that needs to be raised. What, we might ask, if it were a question of 1997 rather than 1927? Would the choice for "model" between the ironic Lu Xun and the irenic Clementi be just as easy to make? For example, what does Lu Xun's snide remarks about Hong Kong Cantonese suggest about his attitude toward questions of "Hong Kong cultural identity"? Similarly, it is an open question whether the vigorous anticolonial sentiments expressed in his essay would translate into support for the development of postcolonial subjectivity. The historical situation, specifically the nature of colonialism, has changed. The more we speculate, the more obvious it seems that those engaged in the task of writing Hong Kong cannot put their faith completely in any predecessor but instead, must recognize their position between two colonialities and invent their own models.

We can broach the question of what these models might be by coming back to the issues that contemporary writing faces. Let me now focus the issues of writing Hong Kong more sharply by considering three kinds of texts: an anthology, followed by two volumes of modern verse, one written in English and the other in Cantonese translated into English.

An Anthology

Gertrude Stein once said, "I write for myself and for strangers." This sentiment is one that Hong Kong writers can certainly share. In a city of transients—and staying for six weeks or sixty years makes little difference—one's audience is always made up of strangers. Yet Stein's remark does not suggest that the practice of literature can ever be a purely personal pursuit, no matter how strong the temptation to regard it as such may be. In however disparate and vestigial a way, writing is always an attempt to define a sense of possible community: if not a community of friends, then a community of strangers. Communication is inescapably a social act. What kind of a community is Hong Kong? That is the question that is eventually posed in writing Hong Kong.

It seems more useful, when considering that category of writing that many are now calling "Hong Kong literature," to raise the question of community rather than the question of identity. The concept of identity is too clear-cut and definite; any attempt to identify a specific Hong Kong literature would sooner or later lead us into a hopeless quandary. A community, on the other hand, can include a number of different identities, and the concept provides more room for maneuver. Writing Hong Kong, we might begin by saying, is marked by an experience of a particular community or cultural space, even if—especially if—that experience is more often than not the experience of a lack or an absence, or of disappearance.

Hong Kong writers have to struggle against many kinds of blockage that leave their mark. The first is economic: writing is paid so little that those who try to make a living from it ("crawling squares," as the local idiom puts it) are, with few exceptions, hack writers. Another, perhaps more insidious kind of blockage is cultural. It is conceivable that the mixed cultural space of Hong Kong should produce the unexpected clashes and collisions that would encourage emergent cultural practices. However, more often than not, this movement is halted by some preconceived notion of East-West differences. Of all the binarisms that keep things in place, perhaps the most pernicious in the Hong Kong context is that of East and West. This is not to say that there are no differences, but that the differences are not stable; they migrate, metastasize. To stabilize differences in terms of East and West is to perpetuate a situation where finding differences becomes a kind of parlor game.

Hong Kong in its amorphousness and diversity often strikes one as being made up of an *anthology* of lifestyles. It seems appropriate, therefore, that one of the first attempts to delineate the elusive outlines of a Hong Kong writing should be an anthology, put out by the translation journal *Renditions*.[4] It is an anthology mainly of writings in Chinese translated into English. As the editors point out, the writings included vary a great deal in terms of literary quality. However, for those who are interested in the possible emergence of a category like Hong Kong writing, the very unevenness of the selections is illuminating. It allows us to see both promising directions and blind alleys.

One of the most interesting sections of the *Renditions* anthology is "Part II: Impressions of Hong Kong," made up of short essays and poems by writers who were "passing through" the colony, including poems by two professors of English at Hong Kong University. Most of the pieces here were written, therefore, in transit, including one piece literally written in the transit lounge—a Hong Kong jail. The writings here, even if they cannot be classified as Hong Kong writing, can be seen as examples of writing Hong Kong, insofar as they provide hints for understanding the social and cultural conditions under which such writing is produced. Consider two texts separated by a hundred years.

The first is an excerpt from Wang Tao's journal, which is an interesting curiosity. Wang Tao was a Chinese scholar who pioneered Western studies in China. He translated the Bible and later collaborated with James Legge in a monumental translation of the Chinese classics. Yet the observations of this scholar on the Hong Kong of the 1860s are, in a charmingly child-like way, very much colored by ethnocentric prejudices. The people of Hong Kong, he tells us, "appear rather stupid and speak a dialect that is quite unintelligible" (37). Describing the guest houses in Hong Kong, he laments the fact that "there are no pavilions and pagodas here. In this respect they are inferior to the mansions of China" (41). The most delicious example of all is his comment on the fancy brothels in Tai Ping Shan and the "sing-song girls" there: "It is a pity that most of them have large natural feet, and that those with tiny bound feet account for a very small percentage, perhaps only one or two out of a hundred" (38). It seems that Wang Tao's perceptions, like his taste in women's feet, are very much culture-bound. What comes through the observations, nevertheless, is a Hong Kong that was already being changed by history into a city that was no longer easily recognizable as Chinese, in spite of the language spoken or the faces of the people.

Wang Tao's journal can be compared to the two poems in the anthology by Edmund Blunden from his volume *A Hong Kong House*, which could be read as a kind of versified journal. Blunden came to Hong Kong as a distinguished English poet, and he held the chair of English at Hong Kong University for many years. The Hong Kong poems deal with the very different Hong Kong of the 1960s, and the tone of voice is very different from Wang Tao's. It is generally sympathetic—and bland. The poem titled "The Sleeping Amah" begins with yet another invocation to East-West "difference": "The East has all the time, the West has none." The poem goes on to half-imply that this "time" is well spent on domestic service: "There she still sits, unknown to us else, in her chair / After the long day's labour." It ends up blotting out all possible misgivings by introducing a universalizing image of humanity: "Like me she falls asleep / Quietly moored upon the warm time-deep." The second poem "View from the University of Hong Kong" describes the boats in Hong Kong harbor ("In their diversity how these boats agree!") and uses them as an image to equate free enterprise with freedom in a Hong Kong that is one big happy family where all travelers feel at home:

> Like a free lively family merrily all
> Are arriving and off again, West or East,
> In the blue-china hall.

Reading Wang Tao and Blunden makes one really appreciate, with the shock of recognition, Claude Lévi-Strauss's categorical dislike of travelers and traveling in the first sentence of *Tristes Tropiques* ("I hate travelling and explorers").[5] It seems that many who come to Hong Kong come looking for a stereotype and are either disappointed when they do not find it, or they end up finding the exotic, which is nothing more than a stereotype of otherness. Between someone like Wang Tao, antipathetic and blind to what is there, and Blunden, sympathetic and bland, we need to find other perspectives and discursive means by which the city could be represented, not avoided.

Those who are more deeply involved in the city write necessarily in a different way. Reading through the selection of fiction in the anthology, one sees emerging from the stories a collective myth of the city, a myth that is sometimes predictable, sometimes surprising. In many of these stories, the main and most powerful character is often the city of Hong Kong itself.

Take the story "The THC Tab" by Huang Sicheng. The story begins by melodramatically juxtaposing the flashy contemporary world of drugs, sex, and loose values with a world of traditional morality and poverty. The main character is a pretty young girl who wants some fun away from the hand-to-mouth existence of her family. She goes to a party, is slipped a pill, and loses her virginity. When she goes home, she confronts the wrath of her mother, a widow who has worked her fingers to the bone to raise her daughters in a moral way. This is, however, not just another story about the conflict between tradition and modernity. There is a twist at the end, where we see the mother's cynical and ambiguous capitulation to capitalism: "'What else is she good for? Rather than let those guys play around with her for free, she ought to be making money for me!' . . . A week later, a fresh talent appeared in the Hong Kong clubs" (107). It is exactly this easy interchangeability between morality and commerce that the Taiwanese filmmaker Edward Yang has called, thinking about present-day Taipei, *A Confucian Confusion*.

San Su's "Hong Kong: 'A Performance Artist's Paradise'" comes even closer to the sophisticated and blasé tone of Edward Yang's film. It is a story set in the milieu of art and the buying and selling of art. The protagonist, the "performance artist" of the title, is a rich man's mistress with many connections in the art and business world. She hits on the idea of putting her name to the works painted by other more talented artists and becomes an instant success, "an instant artist." The story is notable for its avoidance of moralizing. If the "real" artists in Hong Kong are the con artists, then that is just the way it is. She ends her career fairly happily, the owner of a Chinese restaurant in South America, missed by many in Hong Kong, including the countless "nameless artists, who without her patronage can't get anyone to take a second look at their paintings" (83).

Several of the stories deal with the reciprocal illusions that people in Hong Kong and China harbor toward each other. "Greensleeves" by Zhong Xiaoyang is both well written and representative. In this story, a widower from Hong Kong, a successful businessman, goes back to his native city Shanghai to look for a second wife. There he meets Greensleeves, an attractive school teacher who is about to turn thirty and is still unmarried. She strikes the widower as having a certain crispness and clarity about her, unlike the Hong Kong women he knew. They do not exactly fall in love but agree to marry. Back in Hong Kong, Greensleeves little by little turns into a typical *tai-tai* type. She becomes infatuated with her husband's young and aggressive stockbroker, and one night runs off to him to seek the passion that is missing from her life. It turns out—a nice touch that for all his flash, the stockbroker stays with his large family, dependent on him for their livelihood. Greensleeves returns to her husband, and they act as if nothing has happened. There is a muted ending, where we hear Greensleeves's hysteria in the way she compulsively gossips to her husband about, of all things, some acquaintance's act of infidelity.

These stories build up some collective picture of Hong Kong as a city whose will is so strong that it always overcomes individual will. Perhaps the most powerful illustration of this point is the story by Liu Yichang translated as "Intersection." The story, set in Hong Kong in the 1970s, also happens to be structurally innovative. It is divided into short sections, giving it a staccato rhythm, the sections alternating between descriptions of the perceptions of two contrasting characters. One is a middle-aged man, Chunyu Bai, who came to Hong Kong from Shanghai twenty years ago; the other is a pubescent girl, Ah Xing, who was presumably born in Hong Kong. They cross paths a number of times as they go about their lives in the city, but they never actually meet. These two characters experience the city very differently. Chunyu Bai relates everything to the past, to his memories of Shanghai and how life used to be like then. Ah Xing makes everything part of her dreams induced by pop songs and the cinema: the young have media instead of memories. In these different ways, experience of the life of the city is avoided, *faced off* (which would be a more literal translation of the Chinese title). Nevertheless, the very insistent smells, sights, sounds of the city and the violence that always threatens to erupt, either in the form of traffic accidents and armed robberies or, in another way, in the make-or-break speculations on the property market or the stock exchange, make the city itself much more dangerously alive than the two human protagonists. The city, it seems, has drawn the life from them, and this is how it has in turn faced them off. Nowhere is this more obvious than in the context of sexuality, which in the story is wholly vicarious. Toward the end of the narrative Chunyu Bai and Ah Xing find themselves seated next to each other, in the kind of "proximity without reciprocity" that Wong Kar-wai has explored so brilliantly in his films. A trailer for a sex film appears on the screen. That night, Ah Xing dreams of sex with "a handsome man"; Chunyu Bai dreams of sex with her. The story ends with a forlorn image of two sparrows who "flew from afar and perched on the rack. One bird looked at the other and vice versa. Then both birds took off, one towards the east the other towards the west" (101). In "Intersection" no one is at home in the city. East and west here are directions to nowhere.

In the four stories discussed above, the city inscribes itself brutally in the text: taking center stage, enforcing conformity to its rhythms, destroying or distorting affective life. In the stories of XiXi, the city presents itself to us in yet another way. While her stories acknowledge and fully register the demands of the city, they also show how these demands are resisted and deflected, although at a cost. It is a great achievement, especially when we measure it against the odds that must be overcome. Those who go against the city do unequal battle, yet the fight—conducted on the level of mundane events and the small details of personal life—goes doggedly on. If "intellectuality," as Georg Simmel tells us, is a kind of necessary evil required for living in the big city, a way of abstracting and protecting oneself from a too aggressive environment, it is significant that XiXi's characters are neither intellectual nor self-conscious nor obviously gifted.[6] The language in which they are described is simple and whimsical, projecting a childlike tone. More often than not, these characters are marginal figures who either cannot, or do not choose to, protect themselves, with the result that the madness of the city reveals itself in a relatively unmediated way. At the same time, these characters are not presented as heroes; rather, they survive by inventing their own private games, which they play according to certain unstated but strict rules. This makes them look either eccentric or pitiful to others. Moreover, these are not games with time and infinity that take them out of this world, as in Jorge Luis Borges, but games with the mundane that allow them to live in the everyday.

Two stories can be taken as examples to illustrate XiXi's way of writing Hong Kong. The first is "Begonia," whose protagonist Dumb Boy works as a general factotum in an office. The office staff are used to seeing him either with a pail or a mop in his hands and are surprised to see him one day carrying a potted begonia, which he places under a chair behind a door. No, no they say to him in their conventional wisdom. Begonias need sunshine and fertilizers and so on. The Dumb Boy just blinks, as if uncomprehending. We learn later that he has bought the begonia because he is fascinated by a fat caterpillar crawling on the soil, a harmless and "useless" creature, perhaps not unlike himself. One day he is sent on an errand to buy some ice cream. When he returns, he finds the caterpillar gone. The staff explain:

> They said: Dumb Boy, your begonia was being attacked by insects. . . .
> They said: There are holes in seven or eight of the leaves. You're lucky we found it early. We were very brave, and got rid of that worm for you. The Dumb Boy eagerly searched through the waste-paper basket. They said: It was such a horrible, fat caterpillar. Don't look for it now, it's all squashed. The Dumb Boy turned around and opened his mouth wide. (116–17)

The mute ending here has some of the force of Edvard Munch's painting of a voiceless scream.

An even more impressive story, certainly a classic of its kind, is "A Girl Like Me," one of XiXi's best-known works.[7] Its complex implications are as precise as Franz Kafka's "Josephine the Mouse Singer." XiXi's story deals with a character whose work must go unappreciated, indeed, must inspire horror, because it touches on too many things that society prefers to forget. The girl of the title is a makeup artist—with a difference: she is a mortician rather than a beautician, and all the ironies that link beautification and death are told with a kind of macabre, deadpan humor: the antiseptic that permeates her skin is mistaken for exotic perfume, her avoidance of personal makeup is taken for naturalness, and so on. Like many of XiXi's characters, the girl in this story is an unexceptional person placed in exceptional circumstances: "How could a girl like me, with little formal schooling and a limited intellect, possibly hope to compete with others in this human jungle where the weak are the prey of the strong" (109). However, her "ordinariness" also goes together with freedom from more "civilized" phobias about dead bodies: "And I even learned how to take the crushed or shattered bits and pieces of a human body, or the fragments of a fractured skull, and fit them together and sew them up, as though I were only a wardrobe mistress making up a costume" (109).

She has learned her skill from her Aunt Yifen, whose personal life had been destroyed because all her men would run off in blind panic as soon as they found out what she did. And the girl of the story faces the same fate. We follow her as she sits in a café waiting, full of premonitions, for her boyfriend Xia to arrive. They have agreed to go together to her place of work. He says he loves her and wants to know more about what she does. But is love not the overcoming of fear? "And you, why are you frightened?" (111) she asks the corpses she dresses (talking to them is one of the private games she plays). "How is it that a person who is in love can have no trust in that love but is a coward in love?" she asks, gently chastising the young lovers in her care who had committed suicide (111). Will Xia prove to be an exception? The prognosis is not good because XiXi shows us a society whose squeamishness about death is also a displaced symptom of its inability to love anything that is different. The story ends with Xia appearing at the café with the standard lover's bunch of flowers: "They are very beautiful; he is happy, whereas I am full of grief. He doesn't realize that in our line of business, flowers are a last goodbye" (114).

Louise Ho: Writing Hong Kong in English

We turn now to the first of two volumes of poetry. The first is by Louise Ho, who teaches English literature at the Chinese University of Hong Kong and has been writing poetry for many years. Her work, collected now in the volume *Local Habitation*,[8] allows us to look at the question of writing Hong Kong from yet another angle, that of English and the local subject's relation to that language. It takes a certain kind of determination for someone in Hong Kong to persist in the project of writing poems in English. It is the kind of determination that might remind us of Werner Herzog's film *Fitzcarraldo*. *Fitzcarraldo* tells a story about a crazy Irishman (played—why not?—by the German actor Klaus Kinski) and his attempts to build an opera house in the midst of the Amazon jungles. It is an enterprise that involves among other things moving a heavy boat over a mountain. We can leave aside Fitzcarraldo's exploitation of the natives, or Herzog's method of filmmaking that is said to have spoiled the region for other filmmakers and ethnographers, and focus for the time being on the film's mythic dimension. It is not the philosophic myth of Sisyphus that we find, but something else: an urban myth about desire and obsession. As such, the myth can serve as a superb hyperbole for Hong Kong cultural life because in this city—"the last emporium"—it is obsession that brings skylines or poetic lines into being. What Louise Ho writes in "Raw" might have been spoken by Fitzcarraldo:

> Raw as an open wound
> that insists
> on the extremity of pain
> in order
> to reach fulfillment
> is every desire. (75)

And it matters little whether it is desire for philately or philandering, for ascesis or acquisition. In certain situations, to get anything done at all requires extreme measures. In any case, there is no retreat, no place of refuge. The poem titled "Living on the Edge of Mai-Po Nature Reserve" may begin with images of tranquillity:

> This garden this stream these marshes
> A bird sanctuary among mangroves,
> Herons perch egrets glide,
> The hills gather from afar.

But it ends on an ominous note:

> The horizon closes in like two long arms.
> We are surrounded,
> China holds us in an immense embrace.
> Merely the lay of the land. (4)

The too-deliberate insouciance of "merely" only serves to emphasize that it is geography that has played a large role in creating the history of Hong Kong, a history that has also created the subject's relation to the English language.

The extremities in Louise Ho's poetry are masked initially by what seems to be a reliance on English literature as a form of poetic authority. From the title of her volume *Local Habitation* to many details of phrasing, echoes of Shakespeare, the Metaphysicals, and the Moderns are everywhere: the great tradition of English literature is clearly exportable. This is just an obvious example of how the cultural space that one finds oneself placed in gets inscribed into the text. It soon becomes apparent, however, that the references to English literature are there not to show her cultural credentials or to prove that she has earned the right to write in English. English literature figures in Louise Ho's work, we might say, somewhat like the *Don Quixote* figures in Pierre Menard's. It is never a question of working in English literature but rather of reworking the literature. That is why even if the allusions are to English, their meanings get changed by the new context they find themselves in. For example, the project suggested in the title of portraying the city by giving to airy nothing a local habitation and a name works itself out in unexpected ways. In poem after poem, it is the very attempt at naming and precision that *reveals* the frayed edges of a city where nothing is but what is not. This can take a humorous form, as in "What's in a Name," about the city's incongruous sounding name when transliterated into English from Chinese:

> I whispered it
> I insinuated it
> I referred to it
> only as acronym.
> For it rhymed too well
> with ting tong sing song
> King Kong and ping pong. (1)

Here the tones of English are receiving interferences from the sounds of Cantonese. Or it can take a more serious turn, as in the poem about the Tiananmen Massacre, which begins by invoking Andrew Marvell, John Dryden, and William Butler Yeats, and modulates quickly into the problem of naming:

> The shadows of June the fourth
> Are the shadows of a gesture,
> They say, but how shall you and I
> Name them, one by one? (12)

In poems like these, English literature is an initial point of departure that allows the poet to take her bearings on local life and politics, both of which are becoming increasingly elusive and hard to describe. English literature functions less as a form of poetic authority than as a convenient grid against which the metastasizing habitations of the local can be situated.

The fact that Louise Ho chooses to write in English is not in itself a remarkable fact, given Hong Kong's status as still a British colony. What is remarkable—her form of extremity—is that the cultural, political, and personal tensions of the city are so precisely focused by the tensions of her language, by the sensation of "The tautness of the rope / underfoot" (14). Louise Ho's relation to the city could be read in her relation to the English language. For the use of English in Hong Kong by a nonnative speaker is subject to multiple social tensions and difficulties. The nonnative can try to minimalize these multiplicities by mimicking the accents and idioms of the native speaker and hide behind conventionalities. It is always language, more so than conscience, that makes cowards of us all. Or she can choose to explore and exploit these multiplicities and differences and risk misunderstanding or even polite derision. It is in this social and linguistic space in between the conventional and the inchoate that Louise Ho's texts can be situated. The poet, she writes in "Poetry Is," is someone "who shuffles from kitchen to loo / Biting his nails not knowing what to do" (73).

In "Jamming," more challenging and interesting and also more typical of her best work, the very uncertainties of this space-in-between are worked into a bravura linguistic performance. In the process, a Cantonese slang word is introduced impudently as a refrain into poetry in English:

> Oooh, do you think
> she can tell the difference
> Between irony and mere cliche
>
> geeleegulu (21)

To the demand that our language should always be judged by the standards of the native speaker, the only proper reply is *geeleegulu*. The word is Cantonese slang for linguistic confusion and functions in the poem as a way of shrugging off the anxiety of correctness in order to do something different in English:

> Bacon didn't trust it much
> But Churchill thought it rather grand
> On these our very own shores
> Let us make our very own
>
> geeleegulu (22)

For Louise Ho, writing cannot be a matter of purifying the dialect of the tribe, which might have been a valid aspiration for a Frenchman of the nineteenth century or even for an Anglophile American from St. Louis. It cannot be an aspiration for someone in Hong Kong, confronted with a number of dialects without a tribe.

Many of the poems deal with aesthetic themes, but the aesthetic covers a wide spectrum of emotions and implications. It ranges from a simple admiration for the beauty of form in people and objects, in poems like "After Yeats," "Jade," and "MOMA"; to a more complex note about the insufficiency of beauty, as in "Soliloquy of a White Jade Brooch" ("She loved / My white viscosities," but then "She discarded me / For the other / Complex design"); and, finally, to a more marked sense of the responsibility of form. It is at this point that the aesthetic begins to take on some shades of the political. Thus a poem like "Canticle on a Drop of Water" might be read on one level as a formal exercise in the style of John Donne:

> Like a drop of water the will
> Hovers above without contact,
> Adjacent to but always detached from
> Its limbeck which is the soul. (15)

But the poetic conceit of the will as a hovering water drop gives, however indirectly, a certain sense of the floating realities of social and political life in Hong Kong that is a valuable supplement to what can be read in an overtly political poem like "Remembering June 4 1989." Similarly, the poem of hers that captures best the political tensions and ambiguities of the city is perhaps "Bronze Horse," which restricts itself to a careful description of an art object, a very striking piece of sculpture by Mak Hin-yeung. The sculpture depicts a horse's body joined grotesquely to a man's body, the horse's legs "flaying the air" and the human legs dangling from the pedestal. This is not a centaur, which can sometimes function as an image of wisdom achieved through the reconciliation of animality and humanity, but a mindless image of violence and obscenity from which no terrible beauty is born:

> Two motions clash
> like trains
> into each other's velocity,
> two bodies
> countermining,
> two contraries

forced into one orbit:
the unseen body
fully in control,
meets the unseen head,
losing control,
at the neck
of a bronze horse. (40–41)

It is not necessary to translate the image into a political allegory critical of the slogan "One country, two systems." The form can speak for itself.

If form mediates the political in Louise Ho's work, linking language to the city, it also mediates the personal, linking public to private life. This can be read most clearly in those poems where the figure of the mother is an overwhelming presence. For example, a poem about writing can turn into a poem about birth and the mother, partly because writing is also a way of confronting one's own personal history. The past, Louise Ho writes, is "a large collection of images," but then

These do not make a picture
The images are scattered
By constant change
Are not connected
What lurks in the hollows
An absence of adhesion
Like mother's love perhaps. (87)

We do not have to psychoanalyze the image of the mother in these lines. All we have to note is that poetic forms ("images") and the forms of public and private life all share the same quality: a lack of cohesion. History, as Roland Barthes has said, is related to hysteria (from *hystera*, the womb). History as hysteria is what these personal poems adumbrate for us. It is a history that does not present itself as a coherent, cohesive narrative and does not follow clear structural rules. The initial moments of such a history are mired in confusion, even self-loathing:

My nine-months' mother's womb,
With no menstrual issuance,
Blew up with slimy green black bracken,
To grind me out at birth
A deformed lump. (91)

At the end of the process, if one is lucky, a subject may be formed:

> Gestation took decades.
> In the end
> it nearly killed me. (105)

The poems in *Local Habitation* benefit from being read together, but not for the banal reason that they then add up to a greater whole. On the contrary, it is only when we read these poems as a collection that we begin to see their uncompromising fragmentariness. They are like snapshots of a disappearing landscape. There are no grand odes, only episodes. The story is not over yet.

Writing Hong Kong in Cantonese

Evoking the cultural space of Hong Kong through poetry may seem a little perverse because there is hardly a large audience for poetry in this still-British colony. There is no equivalent to a figure like Beidao for China in the late 1980s—for better or for worse. The situation is a little better for those writing in Chinese, who can at least publish their work in the local newspapers and literary journals. I now want to discuss in some detail a body of work by Leung Ping-kwan (better known under his pen name Ye Si). A good selection of his work has been rendered into English verse by the American poet Gordon Osing and published under the title *City at the End of Time*.[9] The translation was done with the full collaboration of Leung and can be used as a fairly reliable basis for discussion about the written text and the cultural space in which it is produced.

A preliminary question to ask is, how much of the Hong Kong situation can poetry, and specifically Leung's poetry, represent? And the answer I want to suggest is that Leung's poetry cannot and does not wish to make any claims to be representative, "to speak for Hong Kong." These forty poems are not a microcosm of Hong Kong society; they do not give us the history of Hong Kong *in nuce*. The easy assumption of a homogeneous social space that would allow a part to represent the whole—such an assumption is never made. As Leung tells us in the piece titled "In An Old Colonial Building" (which also happens to be the main building of the University of Hong Kong), his words are not uttered from a strong position of centrality, "amidst tall buildings of chrome and glass," but from the sidelines, on the margins, in relation to a minor detail of structure, "beside a circular pond / riddled with patterns of moving signs" (31). However, relinquishment of the claim to be representative is not as limiting as it seems, nor is it simply a form of modesty. In historical context, it is more a mark of integrity and a tactic than a limitation, especially when we see it in relation to a situation where group after group is now coming forward to make the claim, more often than not in bad metaphors and with varying degrees of credibility, to represent the interests of Hong Kong. As Leung puts it in "Bittermelon," where this wrinkled and ordinary local vegetable becomes an emblem of what is involved in writing poetry in Hong Kong:

> The loudest song's not necessarily passionate;
> The bitterest pain stays in the heart.
> .   .   .   .
>
> In the rows of flowery, tiresome singing
> you persist in your own key.
> .   .   .   .
>
> In these shaken times, who more than you holds
> in the wind, our bittermelon, steadily facing
> worlds of confused bees and butterflies and a garden gone wild. (105)

This is not poetry as subjective self-expression, nor is it poetry that "reflects" an objective reality; it is not even in any obvious way a poetry of critical opposition. Rather, like the bittermelon, what the Hong Kong poet gives us through a kind of quiet persistence are the real but nonobjective indices of disappearance. Thus in not claiming to speak for Hong Kong in any tendentious way, Leung's work registers much more forcefully the fractures and sutures of a society in the process of mutation. In not claiming to speak for Hong Kong, he is able to show how problematic the issues of citizenship, community, and identity still are and how far we are from a consensus about these things.

There is in Leung's poetry a particular kind of violence that is caught well in some lines by Lucretius that the filmmaker Michelangelo Antonioni likes to quote: "Nothing appears as it should in a world where nothing is certain. The only certain thing is the existence of a secret violence that makes everything uncertain."[10] What strikes me as suggestive here is the idea of a "secret violence," a muted violence, violence with the soundtrack turned off. This is not the violence that we get in modernist literature (even though Leung is himself a student of modernism), which in Charles Baudelaire or T. S. Eliot or Lu Xun foregrounds the shock experience that results from a kind of psychic overload of the human sensorium. It is certainly not the heavily coded violence that we see so much of in Hong Kong cinema and television, with the expected thuds in the expected places. Nor is it like the recodings of violence that we find in the films of Brian de Palma or David Lynch. There is very little that is overtly violent in Leung's work, which in its choice of language, form, and subject matter usually projects a matte, nonsensational, ordinary quality. But this is because it is not the violence of appearance that Leung gives us, but of disappearance and indiscernibilities, that is to say, something both more paradoxical and more characteristic of Hong Kong's cultural space.

Take the opening poem of the volume, "At the North Point Car Ferry," which seems an exception in that it makes use of sequences of surreal images that turn the familiar sights of Hong Kong into a postapocalyptic landscape. The last part of the poem reads as follows:

> Up close to the body of the sea
> her rainbows were oilslicks;
> The images of the tops of skyscrapers
> were staggering giants on the waves.
>
> We came through cold daylight to get here,
> following a trail of broken glass.
> The last roadsigns pointed to rusty drums,
> everything smelling of smoke and burned rubber
> though we couldn't see fire anywhere.
> In the narrow shelter of the flyover
> cars and their people waited a turn to go over. (23)

We have come some way from Edmund Blunden's distant gaze of Hong Kong harbor where ships gather innocuously as if for a family reunion. Leung's poem reminds us more of Jean-Luc Godard's film *Weekend* where a bourgeois couple's casual weekend car trip becomes a catastrophe, and where long queues of automobiles jammed on the highway serve as metaphor for capitalist society choking itself in overproduction and the pursuit of pleasure. But the comparison only underlines a difference that comes out in the last two lines: unlike in Godard's film, which ends up strewn with dead and mutilated bodies, here no catastrophe real or imaginary has taken place. The imaginings of disaster last a moment, after which things just go on as "cars and their people waited a turn to go over." But this is the point: that things can just go on, that no breakdown has actually taken place, that the system can perpetuate itself: that is the catastrophe, the "secret violence," which also means that all apocalypses are now, to use Tadeusz Konwicki's thoughtful phrase, "minor apocalypses."[11]

The violence of Leung's poetry then is keyed in the minor mode, minor in the sense that things do not add up, not even to a catastrophe. What, for example, could be more catastrophic than the Tiananmen Massacre, which has all the ingredients of a major and tragic historical event, after which nothing could be the same anymore? Yet this does not entirely preclude the event from being appropriated and turned into a world historical soap opera. Leung has three poems about Tiananmen, a contemporary triptych that, when seen together, shows well how the minor mode operates. These poems, it seems to me, can be read to be as much about Tiananmen as they are about the highly overdetermined Hong Kong response to the event. Through the use of a simple metaphor, that of furnishing a home, the poems allow us to follow the changing attitudes to Tiananmen. The first poem, "In the Great Square," begins quietly with homely images of spring cleaning ("We'd begun again housecleaning, sorting importances"), which reveal how ramshackle the house has become and ends by registering the sudden physical and psychic shock of the event, particularly the sense of overkill:

> At midnight, Pandemonium! We only wanted to change a few things,
> to draw the curtain over that blemished picture—
> wild sands scattered our signs, thunder blasted our tables and chairs. (69)

In the second poem, "Broken Home," the event is still fresh in the mind but it has already receded a little into historical distance. The tone now is more reflective, and the emphasis is placed not on the moment of shock but on the aftershock, not on the image but on the afterimage, followed by the growing perception of betrayal:

> You say it was always a temporary home, we can build another.
> Sure we can, but our hearts are the furniture.
> . . . .
> The earth shakes and spirits are scattered like glass, broken like flower pots.
> I bend down to lift you from the trampled ground
> but find you and your promises of rebuilding a home with me
> can't stand up. (73)

The final poem is shaped like a kind of postscript to Tiananmen, or more precisely, it shows us how a postscripting or rewriting of history has been carried out. The same metaphor of housecleaning is used, but it connotes something else now, as it is the authorities who do the "cleaning up":

> They cleaned the floors till they shone like trackless water;
> they soaped away the smells of cutlery, until
> nothing had happened; the last smoke went up the ventilators.

Instead of brute force, what the authorities now use is the power of images (what Roland Barthes calls "mythologies"):

> It could not have been a better year, really,
> what with the best vegetables in the markets, undeniable images;
> the nubby cucumbers, the plump new kidney beans won't allow
> insidious interpretations.

And the result? A restoration of old stabilities to blot out popular memory: "The great old furniture, hauled into the Parlor, is History, / solidly in place today" (75). This is not a poetry of protest or indignation: it is worse. By mixing a kind of quiet mimicry of official reasoning with indirect commentary, the poem traces the processes of appropriation and recontainment as they take place. And one of the questions it raises is, which is more violent: the brutal, highly visible, repression, or the insidiously subtle control through images?

Such a question occasioned by Tiananmen has clearly a local address as well because it is this latter, more subtle violence that Leung projects in his poetic texts on Hong Kong. For example, in a poem entitled "Images of Hong Kong," he enumerates some of the contradictions that play such a large part in the daily life of the city, like the man "who studied anarchism in France and came home / to work for 'Playboy,' then 'Capital'"; or the "Beijing journalist who became / an expert on pets and pornography under capitalism." These contradictions go largely unnoticed because of the many resources of recontainment that are readily available here, like the irenics of the mass media, for example:

> One has only to push buttons to change pictures
> to get in on so many trends one can't even think,
> too much trivia and so many places and stories
> one can't switch identities fast enough.

The danger then is of history, too, at least our sense of it, being flattened out into

a montage of images,
of paper, collectibles, plastic, fibres,
laser discs, buttons (33)

—which is like a form of schizophrenia.

What I am calling Leung's minor mode can be related to his choice of subject matter, with its fondness for banal and seemingly unpromising subjects. Risking the banal, as I suggested earlier, is essentially an act of de-exoticization. One of the four sections of the volume is devoted entirely to "Things," where Leung writes about paintings and papayas, potted plants and pears, Chinese bittermelons and pomegranates. If the large themes of life and destiny have been taken over by local soap operas, and discussions of pressing political issues have been preempted by professional politicians, there are still the small subjects and objects left, and these will have to serve. The minor mode can be even more clearly related to Leung's language, with its insistence on the ordinary, its avoidance of bravura and rhetoric, its underplaying of the sensational. There is very little *verbal* irony in Leung's style, no line that describes how the world ends not with a bang but with a whimper; generally speaking, such verbal irony simply tries to overcome on the verbal level what cannot be overcome on the level of social life. On the other hand, there is a great deal of *historical* irony that places things without resorting to verbal accentuation. It is as if Leung were intent in his Thing poems to let objects themselves speak without the distortions of language, as in the poem "Papaya":

I have your words, that you put down on paper,
but nothing at hand to return, so I write down

papaya. I cut one open: so many
dark points, so many undefined things. (91)

However, this is not an attempt to bypass language altogether, which would be a disingenuous enterprise. Rather, it is a use of language that implies the taking of what amounts to something like a political stand: this ordinary language does not come on strong, insofar as a strong language implies belief that one is speaking for the right and the true; it is a "weak" language in its refusal to categorize, to reduce others to a mere object of one's own conception, that is, to a cliché. For example, addressing some local flame trees while riding in a double-decker bus, Leung writes:

I suppose it's impossible to see you as you'd like,
the way another flowering tree would see you.
I stick my head out for a really good look
so I can be sure how your flowers differ from others.
You shake your head as if to say: "cliché after cliché." (103)

It is possible to see in the subdued descriptions and projections of so much
covert violence in Leung's poetry the intimations of a new kind of colonial
space, a space that I have called decadent. The decadent in this sense is
what reduces choice, forecloses options, blocks exits. It is all the seemingly innocuous things that do so much violence to the gently eccentric
characters of XiXi and make them so miserable. A poem like "Lucky Draw"
catches well this decadent ethos of the "last emporium," with all its tacit
assumptions; what Leung describes here is not only the local passion for
acquisition, but also and more frighteningly the inability to imagine any
other alternative:

People carry off their winnings
and hurry to hide them.
I am still here, walking slowly.
Goodbye, sir.
Goodbye,
madam.
I shout from behind,
goodbye,
pumpkin and corn,
take care not to trip
carrying so many things walking.
But they think I am trying to catch up
and walk all the faster. (85)

The question I want to raise now is how in a decadent situation, another
voice could be introduced—a *de-cadence*, we could say, a dissonance. What
I am raising is the possibility of the emergence of a postcolonial sensibility,
and a question about what such a sensibility might be.

Given the very complex historical conditions of Hong Kong, some of
which have been alluded to in the above, the postcolonial does not imply
the decisive leaving behind of the colonial heritage like a style of clothing
that can simply be put on or discarded. When Leung in his poem "In Fab-

ric Alley" refers to the clothing material we can buy in this famous Hong Kong street—

> the thin, translucent silk
> the cotton that drags its touch in the fingers, the coarse
> wool that alters a growing body, the provocations
> in the toes of shoes, the seductions in collars (27)

—he is also alluding to the way in which a whole political system has bequeathed to us the socioeconomic fabric of our lives. It is not a question of throwing away the fabric that has so much of our lives interwoven in it, but of asking "How to go about tailoring something new, / to make it so it wears the body well" (29). Interestingly enough, one of the best commentaries on this poem is provided by a recent story about a Hong Kong tailor. The tailor in question is the appointed uniform maker to government house. On the imminent arrival of the new governor, Chris Patten, the tailor very enterprisingly orders expensive supplies of gold braid and rare birds' feathers in anticipation of a request to make the traditional gubernatorial uniform. But then the new governor decides to break with sartorial tradition and chooses a simple business suit instead. The tailor is out of pocket and in his frustration he has even hinted at suing the government. The joke, however, is on him. What he cannot see is that while it may be the same colonial body that is still ruling Hong Kong, it now wears a new style of clothes, and dealing with such *discontinuities within apparent continuities* requires at least "tailoring something new."

The emergence of a postcolonial sensibility, as we read it in Leung's poetry, is a slow, tentative, uneven emergence, a difficult, messy birth—as is the case as well in Louise Ho's poetry. Sudden jumps of insight and breakthroughs follow long moments of blockage but may also be submerged back into them. There is hope in the thought that when the "blocked places" that the corridors of an old colonial building lead to are knocked open, we will find "stairs down to ordinary streets." But at other times it looks as if frustration and pain are all that are there, and hence the understandable temptation to nostalgia and simplification, to find solace in the timeless and the eternal. Leung's poetry does not always entirely overcome such a temptation. For example, a "travel" poem like "Mirror Lake" with its main contrast between the puzzled human souls who live in time, "laughing and not knowing why / grieved and not knowing why" (117), and the lake's mirror face, with its timeless and calm acceptance of the world, is a trope that comes close to sentimentality, to a simplification of the historical issues. It is as if this mirror face were not (if one may be allowed an obvious Lacanism) a case of the mirror phase, an idealized image of perfection that might serve as point of orientation; there is no such lake in Hong Kong or anywhere else in the world. A very different observation, however, can be made about some of Leung's other travel poems (grouped in the last section under the title "Journeys"), where he shows us that travel does not mean going somewhere else (there is nowhere else); it implies simply the possibility of a change in direction. Travel is not relocation as a kind of escape from local problems; rather, it sharpens our sense of the local and dislocation, for example, in "Cloud Travel":

> Clouds are amazing, but you can't live there.
> Our plane's wings harvest
> > the houses far below,
> > > a mountain chain,
> > > > a coast.
> Our old haunts in the city are left way behind
> > as we enter cloud banks.
> Pretty enough, as I say, but no place to live. (121)

Or take "The Moon in La Jolla," where Leung tries to "translate into a moon of La Jolla Hong Kong's moon," only to find that in this enterprise translation, like travel, cannot settle for or in the familiar, and neither the "imagery of Tang poetry" nor the language of Frank O'Hara can quite get the job done:

> We'll sit together over poems;
> we'll watch the moon come up over the sea;
> we'll be in different places together
> brewing tea and Tang poems, spend
> our nights in foreign lands the closer together,
> the old Tang imagery changed and changing us together. (127)

Postcolonial space then is very much a mixed space, mixed not only in terms of its historical structures but also in terms of the postcolonial's own subjective responses to it. It is marked by the simultaneous presence of different historical layers and sensibilities anachronistically jostling one another, and not easy to separate.

The question becomes one of how to negotiate this mixed space, avoiding both complicity with a decadent ethos and the empty solace of alienation. It would be tempting to read this space as arbitrary and so give up all attempts to arbitrate between signs and situations. Everything then floats and drifts, ending in an eventual drift into indifference. (Is it not such a *misreading* of poststructuralism that gives it so much of its political charm?) What we find though in Leung's best poems is something more challenging, something that opens up the field not by stressing the "arbitrariness of signs," but through a process of what I would like to call the *arbitrage of signs*. In a financial context, *arbitrage* refers to the profit that could be made by capitalizing on the price difference between stocks or currencies that exists in different markets. It involves buying in one market and selling immediately in another. As such, arbitrage is a pretty single-minded activity. What I want to suggest, however, is that something like a transformed mode of arbitrage is at work in Leung's writing. It is not a question of using differences to turn a quick profit, but of turning the cultural and historical differentials that exist in a mixed space to positive use, instead of allowing them to remain as mere sources of disorientation and confusion.

To illustrate, let me turn first to one of the most striking tropes in Leung's poetry, which gives us pairs of objects in a nonreciprocal relationship to each other, as in "A Pair of Pears," "Streetlamp and Tin Leaf," and "A Bronze Pair." All three poems can be read as affective responses to a specific cultural situation. "A Bronze Pair," for example, describes a pair of lovers as two bronze statues:

> how often I've leaned to reach you,
>   caught out in clumsy yearnings,
> wishing you to be a world that bears everything,
>   that frames perfectly my rough edges.
>
> But sometimes you close yourself off completely
>   in a sealed space I can't enter, when,
> through alterations of light I most need your unchanging
>   face, that, in ultimate longing, I imagine I see. (89)

There is more to this image of lovers in the process of being transformed from organic to metallic forms than the romantic topos of unrealizable passion (cf. "Ode to a Grecian Urn" or "Tristan and Isolde"). Through an affective relation, Leung shows us something about social relations: how positions, like that of "lovers," no longer correspond to what they used to be and can be represented only as a structure of transformation or mutation, from the organic to the metallic; and the unfamiliarity of the new (metallic) form indicates that there is a cognitive jump to be made across the gaps of representation. Moreover, this jump cannot be made swiftly or smoothly or without interference; hence the experience of others or of the world or of history is marked by a delay, a numb affective nonreciprocal moment, a hysteresis. Nevertheless, history as hysteresis is still history, and the numbness of affect is at least not an absence of affect, but a kind of pause, a regrouping of energy.

Arbitrage, then, in the sense I am giving the term, might be defined as the ability to find movements and discrepancies in a situation that seems to be fatal and foreclosed, or the ability, to put it another way, to see the humor even of a deadly situation. The work of XiXi again comes to mind. It is not humor of the self-conscious intellectual kind associated with irony, or even gallows humor. What Leung admires in other poets is the talent to laugh, to make light of a serious situation, which is to say, the ability to change the level of discourse. (As Walter Benjamin once said, convulsion of the diaphragm usually provides more opportunity for thought than convulsion of the soul.) Thus in a poem like "At the Temple of the Three Su's," he visits the temple in China dedicated to the great poet Su Dungpo and imagines a conversation with him over food and drink. The temple has become something of a tourist attraction, threatened with being turned into kitsch and used as an object of political propaganda. Leung, playing the Frankfurt School cultural critic, asks some very earnest questions about culture and politics and imagines Su Dungpo's reply. About Su Dungpo's statue that fronts the temple, he asks:

> Does it meet too neatly current
> fashion in politics? And what about the common
> calligraphies and paintings
> billboarding your life? I see—you don't care even to respond.
> I'm just another out-of-towner with nit-picking questions;
> you smile as if to say
> "Who'd have thought in the past's most dismal Double Ninth Festival
> We'd come to see, you and I, such pleasant days to drink." (51)

This humor is neither indifference nor is it political abstentionism. It is, rather, a refusal to answer tendentiousness with a tendentiousness of one's own. It is the same quality that Leung admires in Bertolt Brecht (hardly an example of noncommitment), whom he describes as someone who is very careful not to turn life into a doctrine, not even a heretical doctrine: "You were Puritan to no heresy, living with such ordinariness. / Hundreds of human demons you received in relative calm" (153).

Leung's own best work has the same kind of sly humor that he values so much in other writers. One of the best examples is a set of poems that are disarmingly called "Lotus Leaves" (some of which are included in the first section called "Images of Hong Kong"). The title might lead one to expect a series of elegant exercises in verbal genre painting. Leung quite deliberately chooses a minor form to give us his most thoughtful reflections on marginality, postcoloniality, and the linguistic and cultural problems facing the Hong Kong writer. Usually, the purpose of writing in a recognizable genre is to let the reader know what to expect, to delimit a certain field. In his Lotus poems, however, Leung uses genre to explore and displace the limits of a field, the lotus leaf in each poem functioning as a different thought emblem. Thus in "Leaf on the Edge," he reflects on the problematic nature of working in a milieu that is not at the cultural center of things:

> On the edge,
> I'm nowhere in particular, a smoke-signal in a sandstorm,
> a border legend, a plotless detail in the weeds of history.

The emphasis, however, always falls on the possibilities and challenges of working on the margins. Postcoloniality begins when subjects cease to feel that they need to apologize for their lives just because they differ from more centrally placed others:

> Please don't make an imperial scene, or shout
> anthems to the down-pours; don't pretend, with the breezes,
> to grant us our ditties. Have you ever noted a marginal leaf,
> observed the veins converging like noisy streets,
>
> that challenge your blueprints' rectangles? . . .
> . . . .
> Beneath the winds' quarrels, a hidden song needs other listening. (41)

What Leung calls "other listening" is what I have tried to suggest by the term *de-cadence*. Poems like these, in their quietly achieved imaginings, manage to negotiate the built-in violence of Hong Kong life. Something like a distinct sensibility begins to emerge from dis-appearance.

7

Coda: Hyphenation and Postculture

Hong Kong culture as something that engages the urgencies in the life of its people is a recent phenomenon. Its accelerated development in the last decade or so, I have been suggesting, is largely a response to a social and political situation that has few clear precedents. We need to say a word in conclusion about this nascent culture and the sociopolitical context out of which, necessarily, it has evolved. We can begin by taking some bearings from Frantz Fanon—although we may have to let them go and find different ones for ourselves almost immediately.

Fanon located very precisely the ambiguities of using culture, particularly "native culture," in struggles for national liberation, as well as the ambiguous position of "native intellectuals" in these struggles:

> The native intellectual . . . sooner or later will realize that you do not show proof of your nation from its culture. . . . At the very moment when the native intellectual is anxiously trying to create a cultural work he fails to realize that he is utilizing techniques and language which are borrowed from the strangers in his country. He contents himself with stamping these instruments with a hall-mark which he wishes to be national, but which is strangely reminiscent of exoticism. The native intellectual who comes back to his people by way of cultural achievements behaves in fact like a foreigner.[1]

Fanon's argument, then, is that a national culture—by which he means a postcolonial culture—can develop only after national liberation, and that culture without liberation, or even culture as the privileged means to liberation, is meaningless, reflecting only the intellectual's biased viewpoint about the political efficacy of culture. How then can a study of Hong Kong culture avoid the charges of nativism and intellectualism?

This is possible, I believe, because the situation of Hong Kong is not the same as the one Fanon analyzed. As I indicated earlier, the nature of colonialism has changed in the era of the end of empires and the rise of globalism. The "last emporium" is a colonial city that has acquired some of the mannerisms of the global city—after the last emporium, the mall. At the same time, culture itself in Hong Kong has undergone a structural transmutation since the early eighties. Before that time, when it was seen as a separate or semiautonomous activity that was of interest only to a relatively small group of people, culture in Hong Kong was slow to develop. What has changed now is a willingness, amounting almost to a necessity, shown by a much larger cross section of the people to address issues of culture. And this change of heart is made possible by the perception even among the hard-nosed that culture cannot be separated from more realist disciplines like politics and economics, if for no other reason than the growing conviction, in the wake of Tiananmen Square, that some sense of "cultural identity" is a kind of first-line defense against total political absorption. In this conjuncture, culture is no longer an intellectual mug's game.

But the most radical difference between Hong Kong and the situation Fanon analyzed lies in the concept of "nation" and "national liberation." It is a concept inoperative for Hong Kong, which has never been and will never be in any sense a nation. This is obviously true as regards its colonial relation with Britain, while the relation it will have with China may very likely be no more than an original variation on a quasi-colonial theme. However, if Hong Kong is never going to achieve the status of a nation (on the model, for example, of Singapore), it has already been for some time now something more paradoxical—a *hyphenation*. The fact that it can aspire to being both autonomous and dependent at the same time, where autonomy is in some strange way a function of dependency, indicates that Hong Kong may well be *a mutant political entity*.

Han Suyin once described Hong Kong in a poignant phrase that has since been much repeated, like a popular tune that refuses to go out of our heads, as a city living "on borrowed time in a borrowed place." This phrase, for all its poignancy, has no paradox to it—in that it still assumes a view of history, and of life, where what is borrowed must be returned. It does not describe mutations. Hyphenation has very different implications. It points precisely to the city's attempts to go beyond such historical determinations by developing a tendency toward timelessness (achronicity) and placelessness (the inter-national, the para-sitic), a tendency to live its own version of the "floating world." Whether the delicate balance of hyphenation can survive the exigent demands of the present moment is of course a relevant question, but even China has in effect tacitly acknowledged Hong Kong's hyphenated status by proposing the formula of "one country, two systems," which is a formula not free from paradox. We will have to think of hyphenation then not as a "third space" that can be located somewhere; not as a neither-nor space that is nowhere; not even as a mixed or in-between space, if by that we understand that the various elements that make it up are separable. Above all, hyphenation refers not to the conjunctures of "East" and "West," but to the disjunctures of colonialism and globalism. Hong Kong as hyphenation has to be thought of as the result of a very specific set of historical circumstances that has produced a historically anomalous space that I have called a space of disappearance.

Hyphenation and disappearance raise a number of spatial issues that cultural forms in Hong Kong cannot afford to ignore. Hong Kong's hyphenated status entails a situation where some radical alteration of cultural grids and matrices has already taken place, but in such a way as to be hardly discernible. On the other hand, what is readily discernible derives from the survival of older paradigms that ensure a kind of fake continuity and regulates even our sense of discontinuity. Dislocations now are everywhere, but the novel feature is that we either misrecognize or fail to recognize them. This is what allows us to speak of a spatial unconscious, which is another way of speaking of the elusive presence of colonialism inscribed in Hong Kong's cultural forms. If we pay close attention to these forms whose merits are not guaranteed in advance, it is not a kind of advocacy or nativism, nor a desire to stamp borrowed "techniques and language" with a national hallmark (Fanon), but, rather, a way of thinking through the dislocations of culture.

When we consider some of the major cultural forms in Hong Kong, we see that it is especially through the ambiguities of visuality that spatial issues are raised. These cultural forms either exploit or critique such ambiguities. Take the example of mall space, which by now can be found almost anywhere in Hong Kong. After the last emporium, as we said earlier, the mall. Like emporiums, malls are commercial spaces, but this is where the resemblance ends. Malls do not so much replace emporiums as dis-locate them, through a mutation in the relation of visuality to commodities. Compared to the emporium, mall space is both much more highly visual and basically contradictory. It is a space that allows visitors to believe that they are really "just looking."[2] It manages therefore to delink the activities of looking and buying, but only in order to reinforce them all the more strongly: we no longer see what we buy—we buy what we see. Malls are yet another instance of a space of disappearance.

It is in relation to the ambiguities of visuality that mall space can be compared to the two most important cultural forms in Hong Kong today, architecture and cinema. When we reflect on the architectural examples—whether it is the Cultural Center with its ambiguous attempt at self-definition, or the symbolic landscapes of power of Central, or the appropriations of the vernacular in spaces like Lan Kwei Fong—it is hard to avoid the conclusion that Hong Kong architecture still tends to draw very much on the authority of the visual. When it comes to the question of cultural self-definition, it understands only the false image of power. That is why, as I have noted before, the greater the number of powerful but place-less international buildings that get built, the more the urban vernacular remains anonymous and characterless. In this concentration on prestige and monumentalism, everyday life is not transformed, but only made to look more banal. All of this underlines the urgent need for Hong Kong architecture to develop a critique of space by addressing the problematics of hyphenation and disappearance. The new Hong Kong cinema presents a contrasting example. It starts in the midst of mediocrity, constrained by genre and commercialism. Yet in its more distinguished examples, the Hong Kong cinema presents us with forms of visuality that problematize the visual and provide a critique of space.

When we look at the more important cultural forms that are available in Hong Kong at the present moment, we find there is some reason for at least a guarded optimism. We might note in passing a quite remarkable performance group that calls itself by the name *Zuni Icosahedron* (to underline its "many faces"), which under its director Danny Yung has miraculously been in existence for more than a decade. The group has been accused of avant-gardism and pretentiousness, but it is energetic, committed to local culture, willing to innovate, and eager to defend minority interests. More important, it provides a kind of counterinstitutional framework that gives young people an opportunity to discover their talents. *Zuni* is not just a group of "semiprofessionals"; in fact, one of its achievements is to systematically blur the distinction between amateurism and professionalism. Yet *Zuni*, too, is not without its own contradictions. On the one hand, their productions, which often thematize inertia and paralysis, can sometimes overwhelm by their heavy repetitiveness; on the other hand, the group is well organized, adept at fund-raising and the use of media for self-promotion. These contradictions reflect perhaps the paradoxes of Hong Kong culture. Yet in spite of a group like *Zuni* and other hopeful signs, it must be recognized that the more important cultural forms available are at different stages of development. In the case of writing, there are some very good stories and poetry, but perhaps "the great Hong Kong novel" still remains to be written.

These uneven cultural developments underline the need at this point to develop a critical discourse on Hong Kong culture. Such a discourse will have to attend to the peculiarities of Hong Kong's cultural space, so that its cultural productions may not be judged by false or inappropriate standards. It will have to recognize, it seems to me, that Hong Kong culture is an example of a *postculture*, by which I understand the following: it is a culture that has developed in a situation where the available models of culture no longer work. In such a situation, culture cannot wait or follow social change in order to represent it; it must *anticipate* the paradoxes of hyphenation. A postculture, therefore, is not postmodernist culture, or post-Marxist culture, or post-Cultural Revolution culture, or even post-colonial culture, insofar as each of these has a set of established themes and an alternative orthodoxy. In a postculture, on the other hand, culture itself is experienced as a field of instabilities.

Postculture provides some kind of response to Fanon's skepticism regarding the relation of culture to national liberation, which in the Hong Kong case must be thought of in a more limited sense as the possibilities of hyphenation. The response of postculture is that there is no question of waiting for "liberation" before we can see the genuine development of a Hong Kong culture. On this question, Michel Foucault makes a useful distinction between the political act of liberation and what he calls "practices of freedom":

> When a colonial people tries to free itself of its colonizer, that is truly an act of liberation, in the strict sense of the word. But as we also know . . . this act of liberation is not sufficient to establish the practices of liberty that later on will be necessary for this people . . . that is why I insist on the practices of freedom.[3]

The important role of postculture in Hong Kong today, it seems to me, is to take part in the development of these practices of freedom. Given the kinds of spatial and temporal distortions that we have, these practices are not something that "later on will be necessary"; they are necessary now. Furthermore, the emphasis must be on the *practices* of freedom, which is very different from an *idea* of freedom or an abstract concept of "democracy." In terms of culture, these practices can be located in the development of cultural forms that are responsive to historical change.

Because it is a set of anticipations, postculture can be a preparation for cultural survival. Perhaps in the case of Hong Kong more than anywhere else, there is no chance of cultural survival unless we radicalize our understanding of culture itself. Thus cultural survival is not the same as surviving culture, that is, living within the assumptions of what culture is and stubbornly defending it. Nor is it the same as holding on to a cultural identity. Cultural texts are valuable for cultural survival on the condition that the old cultural myths do not survive in them. Cultural survival will also depend on our understanding of space or spatial history. One of the most important implications of colonialism in the era of globalism is simply that there is no longer a space elsewhere. This means that instead of thinking in terms of displacements, a movement somewhere else, it is important to think in terms of dislocation, which is the transformation of place. Such transformations, even after they have taken place, are often indiscernible and hence challenge recognition. That is why cultural survival is also a matter of changing the forms of attention and seeing the importance of even decadent or degenerate cultural objects. Finally, cultural survival will depend on our recognizing that there is today a politics of the indiscernible as much as a politics of the discernible. One has not completely replaced the other, but each acts as the other's silent support. Whether Hong Kong culture as postculture can survive will depend on whether it recognizes a politics of disappearance.

Notes

1. INTRODUCTION: CULTURE IN A SPACE OF DISAPPEARANCE

1. Italo Calvino, *Invisible Cities*, trans. William Weaver (New York: Harcourt Brace Jovanovich, 1972), 44.
2. Scott Lash and John Urry, *The End of Organized Capitalism* (Cambridge: Polity, 1987); Manuel Castells, *The Informational City* (Oxford: Blackwell, 1989).
3. Anthony D. King, *Global Cities* (London: Routledge, 1990), 38.
4. Sigmund Freud, *Art and Literature*, Pelican Freud Library, vol. 14 (Harmondsworth: Penguin Books, 1985), 90.
5. Walter Benjamin, *Charles Baudelaire: A Lyric Poet in the Era of High Capitalism*, trans. Harry Zohn (London: New Left Books, 1973), 87.
6. Fredric Jameson, *Postmodernism, or the Cultural Logic of Late Capitalism* (London: Verso, 1991), 47–48.
7. Louis Aragon, *Paris Peasant* (London: Picador, 1971), 28.
8. Paul Virilio, *The Lost Dimension* (New York: Semiotext[e], 1991), 31.
9. See Henri Lefebvre, *The Production of Space*, trans. Donald Nicholson-Smith (Oxford: Blackwell, 1991).
10. Gilles Deleuze and Félix Guattari, *Nomadology* (New York: Semiotext[e], 1986), 51.
11. Jean-François Lyotard, *The Postmodern Condition*, trans. Geoff Bennington and Brian Massumi (Manchester: Manchester University Press, 1984), 27.
12. On deterrence, see Jean Baudrillard, "The Beaubourg Effect: Implosion and Deterrence," trans. Rosalind Krauss and Annette Michelson, *October* 20 (Spring 1982), 3–13.
13. Ulf Hannerz, "Cosmopolitans and Locals in World Culture," in *Global Culture*, ed. Mike Featherstone (London: Sage, 1990), 237–51.
14. In Jorge Luis Borges, *Labyrinths*, trans. Donald A. Yates and James E. Irby (Harmondsworth: Penguin Books, 1970), 211–20.
15. See Sigfried Kracauer, *The Mass Ornament*, trans. Thomas Y. Levin (Cambridge,

Mass.: Harvard University Press, 1995); and Walter Benjamin, *Illuminations*, trans. Harry Zohn (New York: Harcourt Brace and World, 1968).

2. THE NEW HONG KONG CINEMA AND THE *DÉJÀ DISPARU*

1. Gilles Deleuze, *Cinema I*, trans. Hugh Tomlinson and Barbara Habberjam (Minneapolis: University of Minnesota Press, 1986), 211.
2. Jorge Luis Borges, *Labyrinths*, ed. and trans. Donald A. Yates and James E. Irby (Harmondsworth: Penguin Books, 1970), 169.
3. Paul Fonoroff, "A Brief History of Hong Kong Cinema," *Renditions*. 29/30 (Spring and Autumn 1988), 308.
4. Li Cheuk-to, "A Review of Hong Kong Cinema, 1988–1989," presented at the ninth Hawaii International Film Festival 1989, East-West Center, Hawaii.
5. Jeffrey Ressner, "Hong Kong's Flashy Films Battle for American Fans," *New York Times*, 9 May 1993, 18.
6. Geoffrey O'Brien, "Blazing Passions," *New York Review of Books*, 24 September 1992, 38–43.
7. See Walter Benjamin, "Central Park," trans. Lloyd Spencer, *New German Critique* 34 (Winter 1985), 42.
8. Quoted in a guest chapter by George S. Semsel, in John Lent, *The Asian Film Industry* (Austin: University of Texas Press, 1990), 28.
9. Quoted in ibid., 113.
10. Paul Virilio, *The Aesthetics of Disappearance*, trans. Philip Beitchman (New York: Semiotext[e], 1991), 20.
11. See I. C. Jarvie, *Window on Hong Kong: A Sociological Study of the Hong Kong Film Industry and Its Audience* (Hong Kong: Centre for Asian Studies, 1977).
12. See David Harvey, *The Condition of Postmodernity* (Cambridge and Oxford: Blackwell, 1990).
13. Paul Virilio, *The Lost Dimension* (New York: Semiotext[e], 1991), 30–31.
14. Virilio, *The Aesthetics of Disappearance*, 54.

3. WONG KAR-WAI: HONG KONG FILMMAKER

1. Henri Lefebvre, *The Production of Space* (Oxford: Blackwell, 1991), 286.
2. Gilles Deleuze, *Cinema II*, trans. by Hugh Tomlinson and Robert Galeta (Minneapolis: University of Minnesota Press, 1989), 19.
3. Méliès's remark is quoted in Paul Virilio, *The Aesthetics of Disappearance*, trans. Philip Beitchman (New York: Semiotext[e], 1991), 15.

4. BUILDING ON DISAPPEARANCE: HONG KONG ARCHITECTURE AND COLONIAL SPACE

1. See Sharon Zukin, "Postmodern Urban Landscapes: Mapping Culture and Power," in *Modernity and Identity*, ed. Scott Lash and Jonathan Friedman (Oxford and Cambridge: Blackwell, 1992).
2. Walter Benjamin, *Reflections*, trans. Edmund Jephcott (New York: Harcourt Brace Jovanovich, 1978), 162.
3. See Diana I. Agrest, *Architecture from Without* (Cambridge, Mass.: MIT Press, 1993), 137.
4. See Greg Girard and Ian Lambot, eds., *City of Darkness: Life in Kowloon Walled City* (United Kingdom: Watermark Publications, 1993).

5. Frantz Fanon, *The Wretched of the Earth*, trans. Constance Farrington (Harmondsworth: Penguin Books, 1967), 195.

6. Milan Kundera, *The Unbearable Lightness of Being*, trans. Michael Henry Heim (New York: Harper and Row, 1985), 248.

7. See Jacques Lacan, *The Four Fundamental Concepts of Psychoanalysis*, trans. Alan Sheridan (New York: Norton, 1977).

8. Paul Virilio, *The Lost Dimension*, trans. Daniel Moshenberg (New York: Semiotext[e], 1991), 13, 15.

9. Manuel Castells, *The Informational City* (Oxford: Blackwell, 1989), 2.

10. Virilio, *The Lost Dimension*, 36. See also *The Aesthetics of Disappearance*, trans. Philip Beitchman (New York: Semiotext[e], 1991).

11. By decadence, I understand a problematics not of decline but of one-sided development. See pages 4–5 for further discussion.

12. See Dick Wilson, *Hong Kong! Hong Kong!* (London: Unwin Hyman, 1990), 146.

13. Alain Robbe-Grillet, *La Maison de rendez-vous*, trans. Richard Howard (New York: Grove Press, 1966).

14. Jorge Luis Borges, *Labyrinths*, ed. and trans. Donald A. Yates and James E. Irby (Harmondsworth: Penguin Books, 1970). See also chapter 2 for further discussion of this story.

15. Saskia Sassen identifies these cities as the new type of international or "global" city. See *The Global City* (Princeton, N.J.: Princeton University Press, 1991). She also suggests that "transformations in cities ranging from Paris to Frankfurt to Hong Kong and Sao Paulo have responded to the same dynamic" of globalization (4). My concern, however, has been to describe one form of insertion into global processes with some specificity, by focusing on the interplay between local history and global processes.

16. Gianni Vattimo, *The End of Modernity*, trans. Jon R. Snyder (Cambridge and Oxford: Polity Press, 1988), 7.

17. *South China Morning Post*, 28 February 1993.

18. Constant, "The Great Game to Come," in *Architecture Culture 1943–1968*, ed. Joan Ockman (New York: Rizzoli, 1993), 315.

19. See Arata Isozaki and Akira Asada, "Anywhere—Problems of Space," in *Anywhere*, ed. Isozaki and Asada (New York: Rizzoli, 1992), 16–17.

20. Henri Lefebvre, *The Production of Space*, trans. Donald Nicholson-Smith (Oxford: Blackwell, 1991), 286.

21. For an account of the relevance of the uncanny to an understanding of urban space, see Anthony Vidler, *The Architectural Uncanny* (Cambridge, Mass.: MIT Press, 1992).

22. Louis Aragon, *Paris Peasant*, trans. Simon Watson Taylor (London: Picador, 1980), 29.

23. Virilio, *The Lost Dimension*, 31.

24. Wilson, *Hong Kong! Hong Kong!*, 179.

25. Lefebvre, *The Production of Space*, 142.

26. Roland Barthes, "Semiology and Urbanism," in *Architecture Culture 1943–1968*, 417.

27. See *Contemporary Architecture in Hong Kong*, ed. Chung Wah Nan (Hong Kong: Joint Publishing, 1989), 10–21.

28. Anthony King, *Urbanism, Colonialism, and the World Economy* (London and New York: Routledge, 1990), 56.

29. Lefebvre, *The Production of Space*, 143.

30. See Philip Johnson and Mark Wigley, *Deconstructivist Architecture* (New York: Museum of Modern Arts, 1988), 68–79.

31. For a good summary and discussion of these issues, see Alan Smart, *Making Room: Squatter Clearance in Hong Kong* (Hong Kong: Centre of Asian Studies, 1992), 30–65.

32. For a discussion of the hyperdensity issue in Hong Kong, see A. R. Cuthbert, "Architecture, Society and Space—the High-Density Question Re-Examined," in *Progress in Planning*, ed. D. Diamond and J. B. McLoughlin, 71–160 (New York and Oxford: Pergamon Press, 1985); chapter 6 on Hong Kong is especially relevant. See also Smart, *Making Room*.

33. Zukin, "Postmodern Urban Landscapes."

34. See the March 1992 issue of *Space Design* (no. 330) with its special feature on "Hong Kong: Alternative Metropolis."

35. For example, they explain that "the fact that Hong Kong lacks urban sprawl today is somehow similar to the walled village's condition against the surroundings. In both cases, inhabitants have chosen to live in a limited area at high-density" (ibid., 58).

6. WRITING HONG KONG

1. Lu Xun, "On Hong Kong," in *Renditions* 29/30 (Spring and Autumn 1988), 47–53.

2. Quoted in Kevin Rafferty, *City on the Rocks* (Harmondsworth: Penguin Books, 1991), 138.

3. In *Renditions*, 29/30 (Spring and Autumn 1988), 26.

4. The anthology is the *Renditions* special volume on Hong Kong. See note 1 above. Page numbers for further citations to contributions in this anthology will appear parenthetically in the text.

5. Claude Lévi-Strauss, *Tristes Tropiques*, trans. John and Doreen Weightman (New York: Atheneum, 1974), 17.

6. See Georg Simmel's classic essay, "The Metropolis and Mental Life," in *Georg Simmel: On Individuality and Social Forms*, ed. Donald N. Levine (Chicago: University of Chicago Press, 1971), 324–39.

7. The story appears in *Renditions*, 19 / 20 (Spring and Autumn 1983), 107–14.

8. Louise Ho, *Local Habitation* (Hong Kong: Twilight Books, 1994). Further references to poems in this collection will be cited by page number in the text parenthetically.

9. Leung Ping-kwan, *City at the End of Time* (Hong Kong: Twilight Books, 1992). Further references to poems in this volume will be cited by page number in the text parenthetically.

10. See Michelangelo Antonioni, *That Bowling Alley on the Tiber: Tales of a Director*, trans. William Arrowsmith (New York: Oxford University Press, 1986), xix.

11. *A Minor Apocalypse* is the title of one of Konwicki's novels.

7. CODA: HYPHENATION AND POSTCULTURE

1. Frantz Fanon, *The Wretched of the Earth*, trans. Constance Farrington (Harmondsworth: Penguin Books, 1967), 179–80.

2. On the question of the visual nature of malls and the relation between malls and cinema, see Anne Friedberg, *Window Shopping* (Berkeley and Los Angeles: University of California Press, 1993).

3. See *The Final Foucault*, ed. James Bernauer and David Rasmussen (Cambridge, Mass.: MIT Press, 1988), 2–3.

Index

ACKBAR ABBAS is a senior lecturer in comparative literature at Hong Kong University. He has also held temporary appointments at the University of Wisconsin-Milwaukee, Tsing Hua University (Taiwan), and Northwestern University. His publications include articles in journals such as *New Literary History, New German Critique, Public Culture, Positions,* and *Discourse,* as well as monographs on modern Chinese painting and on photography.